MW01482440

Theorizing Curriculum Studies, Teacher Education, and Research through Duoethnographic Pedagogy

Joe Norris
Richard D. Sawyer
Editors

Theorizing Curriculum Studies, Teacher Education, and Research through Duoethnographic Pedagogy

palgrave
macmillan

Editor
Joe Norris
Brock University
St Catharines, Ontario, Canada

Richard D. Sawyer
Washington State University
Vancouver
Portland, Oregon, USA

ISBN 978-1-137-51744-9 ISBN 978-1-137-51745-6 (eBook)
DOI 10.1057/978-1-137-51745-6

Library of Congress Control Number: 2016957153

Printed on acid-free paper

This Palgrave Macmillan imprint is published by Springer Nature
The registered company is Nature America Inc.
The registered company address is: 1 New York Plaza, New York, NY 10004, U.S.A.

Contents

List of Figures

CHAPTER 1

Introduction: The Efficacy of Duoethnography in Teaching and Learning: A Return to its Roots

Joe Norris and Richard D. Sawyer

Since its debut in 2003 (Norris & Sawyer, 2003), duoethnography has become a widely known research methodology, through which people of difference reconceptualize their histories of a particular phenomenon in juxtaposition with one anOther. The first publication (Norris & Sawyer, 2004) examined sexual orientation but wasn't even labeled as a duoethnography until republished in 2015 (Sawyer & Norris, 2015a). After a few initial conference presentations, colleagues in attendance requested more details regarding Joe's and Rick's dialogic approach that resulted in a second set of presentations discussing their emergent methodology. By 2005, a name was created (Norris & Sawyer, 2005) and, over time, a series of emergent tenets were articulated (Norris, 2008; Norris & Sawyer, 2012; Sawyer & Norris, 2013, 2015b).

Between 2006 and the present, a cadre of nearly 50 colleagues joined Joe and Rick, presenting their own duoethnographies on organized panels at

J. Norris (✉)
Brock University, St. Catharines, ON, Canada

R.D. Sawyer
Washington State University Vancouver, Vancouver, WA, USA

J. Norris, *Theorizing Curriculum Studies, Teacher Education, and Research through Duoethnographic Pedagogy*,
DOI 10.1057/978-1-137-51745-6_1

conferences, some of which were later published in an edited book (Norris, Sawyer, & Lund, 2012). A second book (Sawyer & Norris, 2013), discussing the methodology in detail, was recipient of the American Educational Research Association's Division D's 2015 Significant Contribution to Educational Measurement and Research Methodology Award and a special issue of the International Review of Qualitative Research (Norris & Sawyer, 2015) contained additional duoethnographies. In addition to the ever-expanding cohort of duoethnographers, researchers previously unknown to Rick and Joe began employing duoethnography in their own research (Farquhar, Fitzpatrick, & LeFevre, 2016; Grant & Radcliffe, 2015; Kidd & Finlayson, 2015; Schmidt & Gagné, 2014; Spencer & Paisley, 2013). Favorable reviews appeared in a variety of journals (Brown, 2014; Chappel, 2013; Gómez, 2013; Latz & Murray, 2012; McClure, 2012; Sameshima, 2013) and others have referred to the methodology in their publications (Davidson, 2010; Denzin, 2013; Ellis & Rawicki, 2013; Reeves, Peller, Goldman, & Kitto, 2013). In just over ten years, duoethnography has established itself as a respected research methodology.

This book, however, marks a departure from duoethnography's original research track, circling back to its pedagogical roots. One of the foundational tenets of duoethnography is Pinar's (1994) concept of *currere*, which considers one's life history, both in and outside of school, as a curriculum. One's environment, media, culture, family members, friends, and experiences shape one's beliefs and practices and by reexamining the past through a present lens and the present though a past lens, one has the potential to reconceptualize one's perspectives and actions. Due to its reflexive, transtemporal nature, currere can be a pedagogical act of unlearning (McWilliam, 2005) as one restories self, creating epiphanies that evoke new meanings of the past and revised visions of the future.

Duoethnography acts in the same way with the additional belief/dimension that if one juxtaposes self with anOther (Levinas, 1984) who is dissimilar than self, one can see self differently. Duoethnographers enter into the process with the intent of learning from the dialogue. Such a stance requires the ability to be reflective, being open to difference, the courage to look at self critically, and a trust that anOther will respect one's ever-changing stance toward self and the world. Consequently, duoethnographers do not merely report their stories; they interrogate them. The quest is pedagogical by design. Duoethnography, then, is simultaneously both a research methodology and a pedagogical act with many duoethnographers commenting on its transformational and therapeutic nature. This collection discusses the teaching of such a process in research methods and curriculum theory courses and teacher education programs, providing the voices of both instructors and students.

Some graduate research students claim that by studying duoethnography they came to better understandings of research in general. Duoethnography enabled them to enter into deep conversations with anOther, gave them greater insights into their own positionality including the complexities of bracketing out/in, made more explicit the researcher/researched dichotomy moving away from the researched as object relationship, and enabled an appreciation of the power of critical storytelling.

Curriculum theory students also appreciated duoethnography's ability "to examine [their] deep seated beliefs" (Lund et al., 2016, p. this text) that fostered honest conversations with one anOther. They came to understand and value the dialogic style of writing that evoked the readers' stories. This approach exemplified a move away from a didactic, empty vessel (Freire, 1986) form of delivery, providing a means to personally interrogate the system in which they found themselves. It is an approach that would live long after the course finished. Duoethnography is a personal form of curriculum theorizing.

Many students in preservice teacher education programs encounter reflective practice for the first time. Being different than the traditional expository essay, duoethnography can be daunting at first, due to its personal, reflective, and dialogic dimensions. But as the process unfolds, many come to appreciate how much they have learned about self and changed in the process. Duoethnography can be considered a pedagogical approach that operationally addresses Cochran-Smith's (2003) belief that:

> the education of teacher educators in different contexts and at different entry points over the course of the professional career is substantially enriched when inquiry is regarded as a stance on the overall enterprise of teacher education and when teacher educators inquire collaboratively about assumptions and values, professional knowledge and practice, the contexts of schools as well as higher education, and their own as well as their students' learning. (p. 7)

Other previously cited texts expand on the tenets and features of duoethnography including this book's companion piece, *Interdisciplinary Reflective Practice through Duoethnography: Examples for Educators* (Sawyer & Norris, 2016) and Chap. 5 of this book (Brown & Barrett, 2016). Rather than reiterating what can be found elsewhere, the remainder of this introduction will take an internal hermeneutic approach

(Werner & Rothe, 1979), highlighting some of duoethnography's salient features that are raised within the chapters.

The Pedagogical Intent to Disrupt and Unsettle

In an era of accountability and standardization, the manufacturing model/metaphor of education is dominant. Students are the raw product, teaching is the manufacturing and assessment is quality control of both the product and the process, with the occasional threat of *performance pay* for teachers and different levels of funding for performing and under performing schools. The banking method (Freire, 1986) with its input of public knowledge to students who integrate it through forms of accommodation and assimilation is hegemonic and over time students adapt to this way of being. In this model students come to regard themselves solely as consumers of knowledge. Norris proposes a continuum (Norris, Sawyer, & Wiebe, 2016, p. 30) inserting personal between public and private knowledge. The personal is a shared classroom space where students discuss and interrogate both public knowledge and privately held beliefs.

Brown and Barrett (2016) state, "Our goal was to develop a practice that disrupts the status quo at both the level of the teacher educator as well as the teacher candidate" (p. this text). However, the shift to democratic classrooms (Henderson, 2001) in which dialogue is the norm can be unsettling. Wiebe (Norris et al., 2016, p. this text) deliberately sets out to challenge "romantic" motivations of wanting to become a teacher. The ambiguity that rests within in the duoethnographic methodology is that while it professes to foster the articulation of the voices of others, it simultaneously advocates an interrogation of those stories, disrupting previously held narratives and unsettling the duoethnographers. Like the characters, Phil in *Groundhog Day* (Ramis, 1993) and Neo in *The Matrix*, (Wachowski & Wachowski, 1999) duoethnographers can expect to be confused as their sense of reality is about to be disrupted.

The Pedagogical Intent to Reshape and Reconceptualize

As duoethnographers destabilize and disrupt their positionality in relation to normative discourses, they surface, voice, and restory fragile counter-narratives. Often these stories present startling new insights about humanity and freedom in a world in which worth is increasingly measured by consumerism and identity framed by essentialist discourses. For example, in "Biracial Place Walkers on Campus", Agosto, Marn, and Ramirez (2015) examined subtexts of different campus locations as active spaces of inclusion or exclusion to themselves as faculty members of color. Agosto wrote, "Our episodes of cultural starvation and indifference are there and painful, but our comebacks are so quick (nourishment as resistance), and therefore so is the celebration" (p. 109). Their juxtaposed descriptions restory the contrived gloss of tolerance on their campus as new possibilities of meaningful engagement. Hummel and Toyosaki (2015) also surfaced counter-narratives in their duoethnography on "relational whiteness pedagogy". In this study, they examined dominant notions of race and gender from multiple complex identities and positionalities. Taking critical and contrasting stances, they explored and deconstructed binary perspectives of identity in relation to cultural constructions of Whiteness: Japanese/European American, male/female, professor/student, straight/gay, inclusion/exclusion, desire/aversion. And Huckaby and Weinburgh (2011) examined the old Confederate national anthem "Dixie" as a context to construct and examine narratives of resistance to new forms of privilege and entitlement in the southern USA.

It is important to note that each of these studies is constructed around a central counter-narrative or narratives. These counter-narratives are powerful in their lived uniqueness and difference. Often embedded in shared cultural contexts and seminal dilemmas, they offer a contingent way of being and making sense in the world. As Edward Said stated,

> The power to narrate, or to block other narrative from forming and emerging, is very important to culture and imperialism, and constitutes one of the main connections between them. Most important, the grand narratives of emancipation and enlightenment mobilized people in the colonial world to rise up and throw off imperial subjection, in the process, many Europeans and Americans were also stirred by these stories and their protagonists, and they too fought for new narratives of equality and human community. (Said, 1993, pp. xii–xiii)

All three of these studies, as well as most duoethnographies, including those of the students of Barrett, Brown, Lund, Norris, Sawyer, and Wiebe, offered the writers as well as their readers a pedagogy of hope and an imaginative third space (Bhabha, 1990) of new postcolonial pathways.

The Courage to be Vulnerable and the Need for Trust

Duoethnography, then, requires the courage to make oneself vulnerable in the presence of anOther and a future audience. Placing one's trust in anOther is risky at the best of times and public classroom environments can increase this sense of vulnerability. According to Lund, "an openness to the ideas and experiences of others, and the ongoing deep critical self-reflection required by duoethnography, require significant personal courage and a willingness to be more vulnerable than with more typically 'neutral' intellectual and research activities" (Lund et al., 2016, p. this text). While Diaz and Grain (2016) "recognized the necessity of initiating vulnerable, critical self-examination around our positionalities, our assumptions, and our epistemologies" (p. 135), Grain acknowledges that such a process can be painful:

> I still struggle at times with the vulnerability of duoethnography, but I see vulnerability as essential to learning. How can we expect students and readers to embrace vulnerability if we are not willing to write and publish with some of that ourselves? It makes for a more honest and transparent research process. (Lund et al., 2016, p. 117)

Breault (2016) concluded in his comparison of an undergraduate class that he taught with a graduate course in which he had more time with his students that the "three-hour sessions made it more conducive to prolonged discussion and the forming of more trusting relationships between both peers and the teacher" (p. 76) assisted in forming the trust that was necessary for duoethnographies. De Loof, a graduate student who chose duoethnography, states, "The other difficult part was to put complete trust in someone else" (Banting & De Loof, 2016, p. 42).

Duoethnography as an Uncertain, Messy, and Emergent Form of Inquiry

An adage that Joe coined and often uses about the playbuilding process (Norris, 2009), "I don't know where I am going but I do know how to get there", applies equally to duoethnography. The research story unfolds in bits and pieces; both the content and the structure develop throughout the process. Norris and Bilash (2016) in this book's companion edition explore how the hegemonic epistemology of positivism and certainty has negatively impacted some students' responses to their teaching. The curriculum of uncertainty is part of their teacher education classes. For them, teaching is far more complex than rocket science as there are many ever-changing variables, their students' lives. Banting and De Loof (2016) explore the poles of right and wrong challenging the quest for right and Wiebe (Norris et al., 2016) teaches to counter the "instrumental and mechanistic approach" (p. 31). Inquiry begins with the unknown, not prescription. Such courses are bound to be uncertain, messy, and emergent.

Such an emergent approach, while a strength of duoethnography, can be daunting for some trying it for the first time. Brown and Barrett (2016) report,

> a consistent theme that emerged was that on one hand the duoethnography lacked structure and explicit direction, which they found frustrating, however, many participants concluded that feeling disoriented was worth it (p. 96).
>
> *At first it was uncomfortable to have vague (ish) instructions on assignments because I like direction. However, I think this strategy and the way you teach is actually how we should be taught (it got easier with time!)* (p. 97).

The ability to trust the process is not a one-off but occurs over time. Breault (2016) would like "to consider how duoethnography might be used in a systemic, developmental way throughout preservice education programs" (p. 78).

Banting, a graduate student attempting his first duoethnography also struggled with duoethnography's emergent nature,

> In hindsight, my analytic structure was doomed from the start because the cognitive distress caused by another opinion created a moving target. I kept suggesting possible headings and topics to scaffold our work, but they always seemed to become irrelevant after conversations. The process required not only a weaving of stories, perceptions, and worldviews, but of styles and preferences. The frustrating thing for me is the fact that duoethnography ensures that you are never reading or writing the complete story. The collective knowledge space is built through our interactions. (Banting & De Loof, 2016, p. 42)

The collaborative approach of duoethnography defers closure, as anOther's frame continually challenges one's own. A dialogic framework, itself, maintains an open form of inquiry that can be disconcerting, at first, for some.

Duoethnography also challenges traditional epistemological assumptions. Lund claims that duoethnography provides a narrative counter to the neoliberal agenda (Lund et al., 2016) and Diaz and Grain believe that duoethnography is "antithetical" to "a system that rewards rationality, sureness, and infallibility" (Diaz & Grain, 2016, p. 150). Lund believes that dialogic practices are "admittedly messy but highly democratizing effort[s]" (Lund et al., 2016, p. 116).

Within a Course/Program Structure

Duoethnographies conducted by students, due to the classroom context, are far more complicated than duoethnographies initiated by researchers. Breault (2016) claims that students are unfamiliar with reflective exercises and Norris et al. (2016) echo this, reporting that many students are not prepared for this axiological shift in knowledge production and that they unsurprisingly find it personally and socially challenging. Within a course structure, not only the course content but also the duoethnographic methodology must be taught. Unlike the traditional expository essay, no previous experience can be assumed.

Barrett (Brown & Barrett, 2016) "felt strongly that the core tenets of duoethnography could provide the theoretical underpinnings necessary for me to help to develop a reflective student-centered experience" (p. 102). He believed that by teaching the methodology, students could simultaneously acquire reflective practice skills. Like courses that require reflective practice components, duoethnography constitutes a new way of being in classrooms. As Breault (2016) ponders, taking a programmatic rather than a course approach may be beneficial. This supports Brown and Barrett (2016) who report that "not all duoethnographic partnerships developed a healthy and trusting negotiated space as one of the tenets dictates, but perhaps starting earlier as this participant suggested will alleviate this concern" (p. 96).

Norris et al. (2016) also raise the concept of assessment. Reviewing and assessing journal submissions is one thing but assessing duoethnographies for course marks raises a new set of issues. While all three authors have difficulties with grading in general, they find their own ways to assess. Wiebe "abhor[s] putting numbers on things and fortunately for [him] [he's] in a program that is pass/fail" (Norris et al., 2016, p. 33). Norris et al. (2016) make duoethnography an option from a number of course assignment choices and Sawyer acknowledges that he has a "hard time with assessment" (p. 33). Wiebe's primary criterion is reflexivity and Sawyer recognizes that duoethnographies are works in progress. Lund et al. (2016) and

Brown and Barrett (2016) do not discuss assessment and Breault (2016) recommends "that if duoethnography is used in the ways described that it be used as an ungraded activity designed to provide readiness or context for future preservice learning" (p. 78). Each seems to find their own way to navigate assessment within the context in which they find themselves.

Duoethnographic Relationships in Classrooms

Duoethnography brings with it other classroom advantages. Diaz and Grain (2016) claim that "duoethnography can also develop a sense of community and alleviate some of the issues of isolation that are shown to so negatively affect graduate student achievement" (p. 150). Banting (Banting & De Loof, 2016) claimed that he "learned many things through this process" (p. 142). He valued the epistemological shift noting that "there is a huge difference between monologues emerging concurrently and dialogues coemerging".

Rankie Shelton and McDermott (2015) consider duoethnography a form of friendship as one gets to know even a long-standing friend a bit better. This is supported by Lund's claim that duoethnography fosters "a sense of care for the other that too often seems missing in the scholarly world" (Lund et al., 2016, p. 116). In addition to an investigation of a phenomenon from multiple perspectives, duoethnography has the additional benefit/outcome of building relationships/communities.

Rigor Through Deep Reflection with Transformational Outcomes

Unlike predetermined curriculum outcomes, the results of duoethnography cannot be predicted. Each individual's unique life history is the source of the transformation. The learning is the ability to be reflexive and reconceptualize oneself through a critical examination of one's stories. As Breault (2016) acknowledges, "Bringing about deepening awareness and understanding is no easy task" (p. 65).

As expected, those writing for this book are confident that duoethnography is a rigorous form of reflection through which transformation is possible. Lund believes that duoethnography's "dialogic approach encourages deliberate self-reflection among students, and a critical examination of the beliefs and values underlying their practice" (p. 112). He claims that

> students report that this dialogic approach, undertaken in concert with anOther, has a way of fostering deeper reflexivity and self-critical understandings—as well as insights about the chosen research topic at hand—all of which are essential as precursors to undertaking any qualitative or interpretive research. (Lund et al., 2016, p. 115)

Barrett (Brown & Barrett, 2016) claims that he was "pleasantly surprised by the thoughtfulness and understandings about what made each individual in the 'duo' fundamentally different. In most instances, the differences were deep and layered" (p. 103). One of his students reported,

> Duoethnography and my partner made me more aware of how my views and perceptions are interpreted by others … it was scary. Everyone has their own story but rarely are we provided with an opportunity to analyze how those stories influence our behaviours. (p. 104)

And one of Brown's students claimed,

> The duo assignment actually encouraged me to self-reflect and express myself and explore these biases that I hold and whether I actually understood what diversity meant. At first I thought it would be simple to define the term diversity however it wasn't until the end of the activity I realized the complexity of the term and it was a challenge to define. (p. 98)

For them and others, duoethnography became more than an assignment; it was a way of learning about self in relation to Others.

Hanson (Lund et al., 2016) not only believed that duoethnography was "the kind of deep conversation I would hope to have with colleagues on a good night out": not only to be engaged, but to really dig into something and find out how other people come to a topic (p. 118) but extended it to learning about research in general. She "realized that duoethnography was one of the clearest examples from my graduate study in curriculum studies of how to examine one's own positioning critically, openly, and personally … interweaving critical perspectives with deeply personal experiences" (p. 118). This approach had positive implications for her own research.

Scott (Lund et al., 2016) recognized that duoethnography "honors the voice of others on their own terms, in their own language and, moreover, foregrounds the subjectivity of the researcher. This can push both parties towards new transformative possibilities" (p. 120). He celebrated this respectful manner of meeting anOther and how this could lead to personal transformation.

Banting (Banting & De Loof, 2016) reported conversations with De Loof "provided many stresses to my lens. ... I feel this revision exemplifies the shift in my lens of right" (p. 60). Their conversations enabled changes in perspectives, As Barrett (Brown & Barrett, 2016) reports, "it was evident that teacher candidates were engaging in comm*unal yet critical conversations* with a focus on the self through the 'other' deconstructing meanings held in their own past and still inviting reconstruction of meaning and stories" (p. 106).

In summary, duoethnography can be considered a way of life, a state of being in which an individual embarks on a continuous journey of self-study with an openness to interrogate self in conversation with anOther.

> This new role privileges neither scholarship nor practice but instead depends upon a rich dialectic of the two wherein the lines between professional practice in teacher education, on the one hand, and research related to teaching and teacher education, on the other, are increasingly blurred. (Cochran-Smith, 2003, p. 9)

In these instances duoethnography provided a process to deeply engage with anOther with the intent of mutual transformations. It is a form of dialogic reflective practice that can be applied not only to research but also to learning environments, research methods, teacher education, and curriculum theory being but three.

References

Agosto, V., Marn, T., & Ramiriz, R. (2015). Biracial place walkers on campus. A trioethnography of culture, climate, and currere. *International Review of Qualitative Research, 8*(1), 109–126.

Banting, N., & De Loof, S. (2016). Right and wrong (and good enough): A duoethnography within a graduate curriculum studies course. In J. Norris & R. D. Sawyer (Eds.), *Theorizing curriculum studies, teacher education and research through duoethnographic pedagogy*. New York: Palgrave Macmillan.

Bhabha, H. (1990). The third space. In J. Rutherford (Ed.). *Identity. community, culture, difference* (pp. 207–221). London: Lawrence & Wishart.

Breault, R. (2016). Dialogic life history in preservice teacher education. In J. Norris & R. D. Sawyer (Eds.), *Theorizing curriculum studies, teacher education and research through duoethnographic pedagogy*. New York: Palgrave Macmillan.

Brown, H. A. (2014). An autothenographic approach to reviewing duoethnography. *Alberta Journal of Educational Research, 59*(3), 525–528.

Brown, H. A., & Barrett, J. (2016). Duoethnography as a pedagogical tool that encourages deep reflection. In J. Norris & R. D. Sawyer (Eds.), *Theorizing curriculum studies, teacher education and research through duoethnographic pedagogy*. New York: Palgrave Macmillan.

Chappell, D. (2013). In ethnographic research, might two heads be better than one? A book review of duoethnography: Dialogic methods for social, health, and educational research. *Youth Theatre Journal, 27*(1), 87–89.

Cochran-Smith, M. (2003). Learning and unlearning: The education of teacher educators. *Teaching and Teacher Education, 19*(1), 5–28.

Davidson, J. (2010). Twisting, turning, folding, and recreating the notion of collaboration in qualitative research… through an artistic lens. *International Journal of Education & the Arts, 11*, 1–5.

Denzin, N. K. (2013). *Interpretive autoethnography* (Vol. 17). London: Sage Publications.

Diaz, C., & Grain, K. (2016). Community, identity, and graduate education: Using duoethnography as a mechanism for forging connections in academia. In J. Norris & R. D. Sawyer (Eds.), *Theorizing curriculum studies, teacher education and research through duoethnographic pedagogy*. New York: Palgrave Macmillan.

Ellis, C., & Rawicki, J. (2013). Collaborative witnessing of survival during the Holocaust an exemplar of relational autoethnography. *Qualitative Inquiry, 19*(5), 366–380.

Farquhar, S., Fitzpatrick, E., & LeFevre, D. (2016). A vision for our children's education: Navigating tensions between mothers and scholars. In K. Scott & A. Henward (Eds.), *Women education scholars and their children's schooling* (pp. 99–110). New York: Routledge.

Freire, P. (1986). *Pedagogy of the oppressed*. New York: The Continuum Publishing Corporation.

Gómez, G. S. (2013). Book review: Joe Norris, Richard D. Sawyer and Darren Lund, Duoethnography—Dialogic methods for social, health, and educational research. *Qualitative Research, 13*(4), 474–475.

Grant, A. J., & Radcliffe, M. A. (2015). Resisting technical rationality in mental health nurse higher education: A duoethnography. *The Qualitative Report, 20*(6), 815.

Henderson, J. G. (2001). Deepening democratic curriculum work. *Educational Researcher, 30*(9), 18–21.

Huckaby, M. F., & Weinburgh, M. (2011). Alleyways and pathways: Our avenues through patriotic songs. In J. Norris, R. D. Sawyer, & D. E. Lund (Eds.), *Duoethnography: Dialogic methods for social, health, and educational research* (pp. 157–176). New York: Routledge.

Hummel, G. S., & Toyosaki, S. (2015). Duoethnography as relational whiteness pedagogy. *International Review of Qualitative Research, 8*(1), 27–48.

Kidd, J., & Finlayson, M. P. (2015). *She pushed me, and I flew: A duoethnographical story from supervisors in flight*. Paper presented at the Forum Qualitative Sozialforschung/Forum, Qualitative Social Research.

Latz, A. O., & Murray, J. L. (2012). A duoethnography on duoethnography: More than a book review. *The Qualitative Report, 17*(36), 1–8.

Lévinas, E. (1984). Emmanuel Lévinas. In R. Kearney (Ed.), *Dialogues with contemporary Continental thinkers* (pp. 47–70). Manchester: Manchester University Press.

Lund, D. E., Holmes, K., Hanson, A., Sitter, K., Scott, D., & Grain, K. (2016). Exploring duoethnography in graduate research courses. In J. Norris & R. D. Sawyer (Eds.), *Theorizing curriculum studies, teacher education and research through duoethnographic pedagogy*. New York: Palgrave Macmillan.

McClure, G. (2012). Norris, J., Sawyer, R., & Lund, D. (2012). Duoethnography: Dialogic methods for social, health, and educational research. *International Journal of Multicultural Education, 14*(3), 1–3.

McWilliam, E. (2005). Unlearning pedagogy. *Journal of Learning Design, 1*(1), 1–11.

Norris, J. (2008). Duoethnography. In L. M. Given (Ed.), *The SAGE encyclopedia of qualitative research methods* (Vol. 1, pp. 233–236). Los Angeles: SAGE.

Norris, J. (2009). *Playbuilding as qualitative research: A participatory arts-based approach*. New York: Routledge.

Norris, J., & Bilash, O. (2016). A journey towards mutualist teaching and learning: A collaborative reflective practice on community building and democratic classrooms. In R. D. Sawyer & J. Norris (Eds.), *Interdisciplinary reflective practice through duoethnography: Examples for educators*. New York: Palgrave Macmillan.

Norris, J., & Sawyer, R. (2003). *The curriculum of homosexuality: The currere of a straight gay male; The curriculum of heterosexuality: The currere of a gay straight male*. Paper presented at the Curriculum and Pedagogy Conference, Decatur, Georgia.

Norris, J., & Sawyer, R. (2004). Null and hidden curricula of sexual orientation: A dialogue on the curreres of the absent presence and the present absence. In L. Coia, M. Birch, N. J. Brooks, E. Heilman, S. Mayer, A. Mountain, & P. Pritchard (Eds.), *Democratic responses in an era of standardization* (pp. 139–159). Troy, NY: Educators' International Press.

Norris, J., & Sawyer, R. (2005). *Towards the dialogic and critical engagement of duoethnography for transformative curriculum: An interactive discussion of methodology*. Paper presented at the Curriculum and Pedagogy Conference, Oxford, Ohio.

Norris, J., & Sawyer, R. (2012). Toward a dialogic methodology. In J. Norris, R. D. Sawyer, & D. E. Lund (Eds.), *Duoethnography: Dialogic methods for social, health, and educational research* (pp. 9–39). New York: Routledge.

Norris, J., & Sawyer, R. (2015). Guest editors. *International Review of Qualitative Research, 8*(1), 1–143.

Norris, J., Sawyer, R. D., & Lund, D. (Eds.). (2012). *Duoethnography: Dialogic methods for social, health, and educational research*. New York: Routledge.

Norris, J., Sawyer, R. D., & Wiebe, S. (2016). Teaching through duoethnography in teacher education and graduate curriculum theory courses. In J. Norris & R. D. Sawyer (Eds.), *Introduction the efficacy of duoethnography in teaching and learning: A return to its roots*. New York: Palgrave Macmillan.

Pinar, W. (1994). The method of Currere (1975). In W. Pinar (Ed.), *Autobiography, politics and sexuality: Essays in curriculum theory 1972–1992* (pp. 19–27). New York: Peter Lang.

Ramis, H. (Director). (1993). *Groundhog Day*. Culver City: Columbia Pictures.

Rankie Shelton, N., & McDermott, M. (2015). Duoethnography on friendship. *International Review of Qualitative Research, 8*(1), 68–89.

Reeves, S., Peller, J., Goldman, J., & Kitto, S. (2013). Ethnography in qualitative educational research: AMEE Guide No. 80. *Medical Teacher, 35*(8), e1365–e1379.

Said, E. W. (1993). *Culture and imperialism*. New York: Alfred A Knopf.

Sameshima, P. (2013). Duoethnography. Understanding qualitative research & duoethnography: Promoting personal and societal change within dialogic self-study. *Journal of the Canadian Association for Curriculum Studies, 11*(1), 174–190.

Sawyer, R., & Norris, J. (2013). *Understanding qualitative research: Duoethnography*. New York: Oxford University Press.

Sawyer, R., & Norris, J. (2015a). Hidden and null curricula of sexual orientation: A duoethnography of the absent presence and the present absence. *International Review of Qualitative Research, 8*(1), 5–26.

Sawyer, R., & Norris, J. (2015b). Duoethnography: A retrospective 10 years after. *International Review of Qualitative Research, 8*(1), 1–4.

Sawyer, R. & Norris, J. (2016). *Interdisciplinary reflective practice through duoethnography: Examples for educators*. New York: Palgrave Macmillan.

Schmidt, C., & Gagné, A. (2014). Diversity and equity in an educational research partnership: A duoethnographic inquiry. *IJE4D Journal, 3*, 1–19.

Spencer, C., & Paisley, K. (2013). Two women, a bottle of wine, and the bachelor: Duoethnography as a means to explore experiences of femininity in a leisure setting. *Journal of Leisure Research, 45*(5), 695.

Wachowski, A., & Wachowski, L. (Dirctors). (1999). *The Matrix*. Burbank, CA: Warner Brothers.

Werner, W., & Rothe, P. (1979). *Doing school ethnography*. Edmonton: Department of Secondary Education, University of Alberta.

CHAPTER 2

Teaching through Duoethnography in Teacher Education and Graduate Curriculum Theory Courses

Joe Norris, Richard D. Sawyer, and Sean Wiebe

The Conversation

Joe: My teaching at the university level has always been underpinned by the belief that the medium is the message (McLuhan, 1964), that there are multiple ways of knowing, and that each media used, word, number, image, gesture, and sound (McLeod, 1987) influences its meaning and vice versa. While I recognize the value of expository writing, I have questioned its hegemony in teaching, assessment, and research dissemination (Norris, 2008). In the early 1990s I began to invite students to explore a number of different ways of presenting their final assignments, the expository essay being but one. Over the years I have received recorded music, quilts, stained glass, collages, sculptures, paintings, and movie reviews and programs, all with metacognitive logs, articulating the meanings that

J. Norris (✉)
Brock University, St. Catharines, ON, Canada

R.D. Sawyer
Washington State University Vancouver, Vancouver, WA, USA

S. Wiebe
University of Prince Edward Island, Charlottetown, PE, Canada

J. Norris, *Theorizing Curriculum Studies, Teacher Education, and Research through Duoethnographic Pedagogy*,
DOI 10.1057/978-1-137-51745-6_2

emerged through the art-making processes. Some adorn my office wall. I was amazed at the deep thinking that was conveyed and many students claimed that they better understood the material through these types of assignments.

Also, based upon Pinar's (1994) concept of currere or curriculum of life, I wanted to expand the notion of curriculum beyond that of schooling. We learn from our experiences and the culture in which we live, and these, too, are part of our curriculum. Using the concept of reconceptualization (Pinar, 1981), in a graduate curriculum theory course I taught students how to look at themselves transtemporally. They looked at how the past shaped the present, how the present could reconceptualize the past and how both could create a newly imagined future. We watched *Groundhog Day* (Ramis, 1993), asking what was Phil's curriculum that took him from being a misanthrope to that of altruism. The character's life could be considered a remedial classroom of sorts. We applied to our own lives asking what life experiences informed our present beliefs, and, in so doing, expanded our definition of curriculum beyond that of subject matter. In some ways, this approach was autoethnographic (Bochner & Ellis, 2002) with an emphasis on the changes of a particular phenomenon over time.

One assignment option was take a look at their curriculum of X. A number of students chose to reexamine their own curriculum of something including fitness, body image, and perceptions of gender. Others did movie reviews in which the character went through major life changes. One student compared *The Last Samurai* (Zwick, 2003) and *Dances with Wolves* (Costner, 1990), claiming that they shared a basic plot structure. Despair and cultural displacement led the characters toward change. For these and others, their understanding of curriculum expanded. Duoethnography is a dialogic form of currere.

Sean: Right at the beginning of a course called *Integrated Foundations*, I introduce students to duoethnography because at this point in their program they have taken a number of courses together within the Univerity of Prince Edward Island (UPEI) cohort model. Students tend to feel like they already know one another, especially in Prince Edward Island (PEI), where the common story is "We are a friendly place, we all get along." And that sense of how the "we" is constructed needs to be troubled. Students normally have vague and dualistic ideas about difference: white/black, male/female, rich/poor. Few understand their unique particularities and how events in their life stories have shaped who they are and their perceptions of others. Doing a duoethnography disrupts their comfortable communities that normally evolve through sameness. By asking them to refocus on their differences, I hope to enrich their experience of another. One aim of the *Integrated Foundations* course is to assist preservice teachers untangle themselves from some of the normative ideals and grand narratives of teaching (Britzman, 1998; Freitas & McAuley, 2008).

In explaining the basics of duoethnography, I emphasize that the *site* of the research is their life story, and the *data* they will be focusing on are how the events of that story have shaped who they are. Using research language challenges them, but when I break it down into these two emphases, site and data, students can usually follow. Archeological imagery is helpful: Students travel to the site (the life story), then start to dig (gather data through dialogue), then pay attention to the differences in one another's stories.

Lastly, I ask them to be creative in the representation of what they've done; this is an invitation to share their dialogues in an aesthetic way. In my explanations I use the terms *theoria*, *praxis*, and *poiesis*, and suggest that representing their knowing (*theoria*) through *poiesis* (art-making) enriches what they know, and creates a third space for how their knowing/making changes them and others (*praxis*).

Joe: Similarly, I use Gadamer's (1975) concept of translation, explaining that the third space is between the media chosen.

Sean: Praxis, of course, means doing. Preservice teachers often think of their practicum as *praxis* and their course work as *theoria*. In duoethnography the knowing/doing binary changes: the experience of doing duoethnography changes the knowing of who they are. My hope is that this changes what it means to be a teacher.

Rick: In the teacher preparation course that I teach I work with preservice teachers who have not traveled far, so they've been socialized into a particular culture that doesn't necessarily value diversity. Many of these students also identify with schools and the overall process of education. My goal in using duoethnography is to encourage my students to develop a more complex and diverse lens. I want them to start seeing education and schooling as a construction of which they are part. Sean, I like how you said that you want your students to see themselves as the site of the instruction. They filter the teaching and learning experience through who they are—their beliefs and values that allow them to either critique or reinforce the status quo.

And then, similar to what you are doing Joe, *currere* is a central construct as we examine life as text in a transtemporal way, using the past to reconceptualize their view of the present and the present to reconceptualize their view of the past. The class is partly about life as curriculum. I want them to have agency and recognize that their story is a construction and thus to expand their notion of curriculum is not very narrow and just confined. Similar to the work of Ted Aoki (Aoki, Pinar, & Irwin, 2005a), I want them to experience in a conscious way how curriculum is lived and embodied. And I also want them to see that a dialogic curriculum involves democracy and that it is never finished or certain. So this is all background and some of my goals.

Joe: What I find interesting in listening to your stories and comparing them to mine is that I am no longer in a faculty of education. I am no longer in a teacher education program, although I do call my program a *pre* preservice teacher education program because I teach the teaching of drama. I have not had much opportunity to teach education students for about eight years, although in the summer of 2014 I taught a graduate course on curriculum theory at the University of Alberta and one of the chapters in this book was written by students from that class. In the falls of 2014 and 2015 I taught a research methods course for the Social Justice and Equity Studies program at Brock University but not much time was spent on duoethnography

So my recent teaching experiences with duoethnography are limited and I don't see myself doing more in the near future. So, for me, I'm drawing on experiences of a number of years ago. So as one with a more distant perspective, I would say Rick is looking at currere both outside and within the school system, Sean seems to be more on within the school system focusing on teacher identity, and I've tended to focus more on outside of school, if we want to make that a distinct comparison.

Sean: Because I have an audience of teachers, it's probably fair to describe their work as a *within* school process, but as students seek to understand the history of their construction of who they are, I tend to think of that as an *outside* the school process. There is a tension here—as you both have written about—because positioned as an actor or character in the classroom setting, student/teacher life histories unfold differently, as if significant life moments cannot be interpreted without reference to becoming a teacher. As an aside, I like the simplicity of the phrase life history, or life writing. Chambers, Hasebe-Ludt, Leggo, and Sinner (2012) have simplified the language of *currere*; duoethnography is also well-named, as the name is a straightforward representation of what is happening.

Rick: Yes, given that I'm working with people who want to be teachers, I focus on their classroom lives. But I also consider their curricular lives within and outside the classroom something of a dialogue, and I want them to see how they live in an in-between space that connects to what they do with students inside the classroom. And of course their students have their own life histories as well. I draw on Jean Clandinin and Michael Connelly's (2000) notion of curriculum and the history of the discipline, so curriculum is a narrative with multiple transtemporal intersections. And I want the students to understand that their views of curriculum are probably grounded in something that they need to deconstruct to work equitably with people different from themselves.

Joe: I guess for me, not implying that one is better or worse, I am trying to pull away from school and look at the curriculum of life beyond the school system. I wanted to break the teacher conversation or disrupt it because I found that when I taught practicing teachers, the students would say, "Well, you know what happened this year" or "you know what happened last week", and they would get wrapped up in their story and their ideology. While they needed to vent there wasn't that critical reflection that was necessary for the course. Going back to their life histories gave them distance from the immediate. Geertz's (1974) concepts of experience-near and experience-far, which are a better set of terms than objective and subjective, apply here. I deliberately pulled away from school experiences because they were too close to it and most of the course was actually about school experiences. The outside of school currere brought a wider perspective.

Rick: I'm trying to help my students construct a notion of who they are as a teacher—of who they are becoming—and to pull them away from normative views of schooling and curriculum. So, the emphasis is outside the classroom but intertwined closely with their classroom identity and the construction of that identity.

Joe: The courses that I taught had teachers with 5, 10, or 20 years of teaching experience. Their identities were well established. To directly challenge them could generate resistance. The distance of life in general was an easier way in. Rick, in your case there experiences are very recent, correct?

Rick: Right. They are becoming teachers and this course is at the beginning of their program. They haven't even gone into a secondary classroom yet. So their notion of self is tied to induction by observation (Lortie, 1975)—tied to their own history of teaching and learning.

Joe: So, an important distinction to make throughout this chapter is whether we are referring to preservice or in-service teacher teachers. Sean, do you teach mostly preservice or both?

Sean: Duoethnography is something I do mostly with preservice teachers, but I did teach a graduate course last January where I gave in-service teachers the choice to do a duoethnography. In my preservice teacher education course the whole class experienced it over three sessions (nine hours total of class time), and, because it was right at the beginning of the course, doing the duoethnography was critical to how the class unfolded.

Rick: I've done both as well and there has been a difference in working with preservice and in-service teachers. Maybe we can explore this further because I think that there are important distinctions between the two groups.

Joe: I have no experience with preservice in relation to duoethnography, but one of the things that you raise, Sean, which I think is an important one, is the concept of choice. For me, I typically give four assignment choices: They could do a traditional paper on a course concept. For those who needed the security of something they knew well could go that way. Another choice was an arts-based approach, like collages with metacognitive logs. Two students in the 2015 Research Methods course did collages, another an interpretive dance, and another wrote a scripted hypothetical conversation with the literature authors. A third was *currere* of a character in a book, novel, or movie. The fourth choice was duoethnography. Two groups of students in the 2014 curriculum theory course chose the duoethnography option for two reasons: one, they wanted to do a paper with somebody else, they were tired of doing an assignment alone; and, two, they sort of embraced the idea of wanting to learn from someone else. So it was both the process and the product that seemed to draw them to conducting a duoethnography as their final assignment.

Sean: My students tend to have an overly romantic notion of why they want to become teachers and some courses in our Bachelor of Education[1] program nurture this, so students have heard things like, "If you don't love children, you can't be a teacher." Students respond to these overly optimistic and intensely positive experiences of being a teacher. I think this relates to what you are saying, Rick, about a sense of normativity. In my integrated foundations course, doing a duoethnography is an opportunity to disrupt that. Previous to calling this assignment a duoethnography, I was working with a Deborah Britzman (2009) chapter that asked, "Why would anybody want to be a teacher?" I wanted students to really question their inspirations and aspirations for wanting to be teachers, hoping they would see in each other's life constructions what was pulling them, what was constructing who they were, and hoping they would find something apart from this romanticized story of being a teacher.

Rick: There are all sorts of normative forces at play right now: the notion that there is a "best practice" for all, that the dominant discourse doesn't really need to be unpacked, the notion of expert knowledge and who owns that knowledge, what counts as knowledge, how can that be tested, and the need for accountability. In my program a lot of people treat the preservice teachers completely as novices who are not bringing in any previous knowledge or experience.

Joe: After listening to both of you, I found a third reason why my students chose duoethnography as an assignment. Sean, you mentioned that you give them a duoethnography to read. Therein lies the third reason. I gave my students an earlier version of Rick's and my update piece on sexual orientation (Sawyer & Norris, 2015) and they were just blown away by it. They liked both the content and the form; they loved the narrative style; they thoroughly said that they began to think of their own stories (like duoethnographers do) as they read that story, and thought it was such a great read that they wanted to write one like it. This was articulated in all three graduate courses.

Sean: What my students responded to, which was new to them, is that their site for the collection of data was right there in the person's life story. The immediacy was a surprise, also that they were generating the data themselves through dialogue. Even though my students are in their fifth year of university, most of them have never considered the idea that the construction of a life story can be analyzed as part of the research process. They learn that dialogue can be more than chatting—in between them, in that third space, something can emerge that is a co-constructed analysis of each other's stories where synthesis is not the objective, and that is counterintuitive. Students are surprised when I ask them to focus on their differences. In research difference *is* counterintuitive. With coding, for example, themes emerge from similarity and frequency. In my integrated foundations course, I want them to understand alternate ways of being and knowing, to question knowledge, policies, or practices that are justified because of a sense of what is held in common.

Joe: Imagine if the common phrase "Oh, we have so much in common" was replaced with "Oh, we have so much in difference." Norm referencing is hegemonic with difference considered an outlier. There are major axiological dimensions of the normal curve that need to be addressed, too much for this chapter. However, because difference is one of the pillars of duoethnography, the methodology it challenges is normative structures.

Rick: Students want to make sense of things: I understand that. That resonates with a part of my past, as opposed to "stop making sense". Sean, you talk about the counterintuitive and that we start to challenge ourselves when something does not make sense or is not consistent with our frameworks. Because duoethnography is founded on the premise of learning from difference, it disrupts normative views of our lives and histories.

So, how do you set it up, Sean, if you are going to use duoethnography in the classroom?

Sean: I mentioned earlier the archeological metaphor where I emphasize that the *site* of the research is their life story, and the *data* they will be focusing on are the events of that story. But I'm also asking them to take particular notice of places of difference, and to articulate those differences, to leave them unresolvable. An important part of the setup is students knowing that it is okay to have unresolvable differences.

Joe: And this is more than epistemological. Reason and Hawkins (1988) discuss in their chapter *Storytelling as Inquiry* that this type of research has elements of both express and explain. The expository essay explains. In my work with playbuilding (Norris, 2009) we emphasize expression. We provide unresolvable scenes with thesis and antithesis and invite the audience to form and articulate their own unique synthesis, albeit ever so fleeting. Extending Barone's (1990) perspective on the narrative, expressions evoke, creating dialogue, while the act of explaining tends to privilege the author's perspective. Smith and Heshusius (1986) caution against closing down conversations and, coupled with Rosenblatt's readers' response theory, texts that bring readers into the conversation expand; they don't shut down. By structuring the narrative in a dialogical format duoethnography brings more of the reader into the process, making it a different axiological approach.

Sean: When I use the terms *theoria*, *praxis*, and *poiesis*, the key for me is to avoid synthesis. So, when I invite students to poke and prod in their partner's life text, they have to resist that tendency to seek commonality. Commonality is a form of closure, and the trouble is there is no letting go of the ownership. Closure is always a temptation because it feels like success. The assignment is complete. "What next, prof? Do you have any other quaint assignments for us?" Resisting closure is one way duoethnography is like currere, particularly in the analytical phase—so I say to students, "When you're looking at the text of another person, you become its *deconstructor* and *reconstructor*". We tend to feel like we own our life stories, that it is a single authored text. But when we let go of our text, when we share the deconstruction and reconstruction, it is easier to resist closure.

Joe: Could I add the word muse?

Sean: I like that.

Joe: I also say, "create texts that will haunt you and your readers for eternity. In so doing, we become each other's muse."

Rick: I can see that there is a new dialogic space and people are imagining something new based on the dialogue.

Sean: The basic overview is looking for differences; being the site of each other's research; listening to the other person's story without doing any analysis at first; then going back to that text and together constructing an analysis of this person as a becoming teacher. Lastly, they are avoiding the grand narratives of teaching, especially the romantic ones, like I mentioned before, avoiding those tropes of "I want to change the world" or "I really love children", that kind of thing.

Joe: Building upon Weizenbaum's (1984) concept of "unbounded questions" Henderson (1992) in *Reflective teaching: Becoming an inquiring educator* talks about their value in guiding practice. *Such* questions can never be fully answered but need to be always asked. For example, Scudder (1968) asks, "How can one teach with authority as an expert in a discipline, without violating the integrity of students?" (p. 133). This is one that I still ask daily. I invite my students to go on such quests. "To dwell", as Aoki (2005b) would say, "in the question" (p. 156), with the recognition that it is complex and unbounded. It's a journey I think we should all enter into. Sean, unbounded links to your concept of uncertainty.

Sean: I should also mention that I ask them to represent what they discover in an aesthetic way. They could write a series of poems or create a dramatic piece to present. There is no limit here, but there are two things I emphasize: I want them to be able to reveal and feel comfortable revealing because in the artistic form they're saying this isn't exactly who we are, but something else that we've created together, and that nicely demonstrates something that's often more intensely personal than they realized, and gives them a form of safety because they're now creating art as the final representation.

Joe: Sean, it seems that you start with the abstract and I start with an example. Rick?

Rick: So my course is part of a broader curriculum, not just about duoethnography. The thread that this relates to is embodied curriculum. In the class we begin with some theory, with readings by Ted Aoki (2005a),

Paolo Freire (1986), Louise Rosenblatt (1978), and James Macdonald (1995). We examine the lived curriculum, the spiritual curriculum, and try to reframe our view of justice to begin to discuss larger processes. Then we examine Clandinin and Connelly on curriculum (1988, 1992, 1995) and shift into arts integration and examine an article that you wrote, Sean (Wiebe et al., 2007)—and at this point the students are swimming in a sea of new ideas (which as a temporary state, I consider a good thing).

Joe: Like Phil in Groundhog Day.

Rick: So we start somewhat abstractly, but I then ask the students to bring in a photograph without any words as a metaphor for what they think curriculum is. We all, including myself, do this and then present our metaphor in class. I organize them into pairs and initially they are not allowed to explain their own image. Someone else has to interpret their own image for them. And then we begin to develop an elaborate class text for curriculum. This text becomes the basis for a discussion about difference and multiple ways of knowing. This project shares with photovoice an emphasis on participatory research and critical consciousness (Wang & Burris, 1997), but differs by its greater emphasis on learning from difference and dialogism (Bhabha, 1991, 1994). We don't try to combine these different views into one singular view of curriculum—which is impossible because there are too many different views of curriculum to weave together into a single coherent stable meaning. The view of curriculum is so complex that we can't quite wrap our minds around it.

Then, as a class, we move into the topic of duoethnography more explicitly as a way to begin to deconstruct our views of curriculums. However, in many ways, we have already been living in a duoethnographic state. I then have them read at home the duoethnography on beauty (Rankie Shelton, & McDermott, 2011). This is a good choice because they all understand that cultural images of beauty are a construction. The important part is that they know that as teachers they do not want to have their views of their children framed by cultural images of beauty. We read the duoethnography on beauty and they are speechless at first, followed by a rich conversation.

Joe: What percentage of your students are female?

Rick: Sixty percent and this is in our secondary program. So having this many, in a way, is a good thing.

Joe: How do the males respond to the beauty one?

Rick: I think that the assignment/topic does resonate more with the women. The males did it as well. Part of their response, though, was contingent on how they are positioned in terms of how they identify with processes of education, and, to a certain extent, many of them are -counter-identifiers. Many of them want to change the system and so I think they get it, not about beauty per se, but that it is a construction and that they are interested in those ideas and that many of them are intellectual. But this topic appeared to be gendered in different ways and the women found that topic very interesting.

Joe: What I like about this example is that you've chosen is one that will personally resonate but not necessarily from a school perspective.

Rick: Right. It's that tension between being inside and outside school.

Sean: What you said, Rick, about how your students encounter a number of curriculum theories before they move into duoethnography reminds me that before beginning my course with duoethnography, students read Martha Nussbaum's (2009) *Education for Profit, Education for Freedom.* She helps students see skill acquisition for employment as part of a larger discourse, and they begin to deconstruct their main assumptions about education, understanding it as more and less than what they thought it might be. It's helpful for them to be thinking about how they are often complicit in these discourses, reproducing certain kinds of privileges, certain kinds of community power relations, and then when we move to duoethnography, they more readily see that complicity in each other's life stories.

Rick: Joe, you've talked about this before—that we don't really consider duoethnography being about epistemology but also about ontology. How do you go beyond epistemology?

Joe: As stated earlier Reason's and Hawkin's concept of express and explain help, although they are not a completely accurate division. Still, I regard epistemology as explaining with expressing being ontological. When I read a story written by others, I enter into their live-worlds, I can feel things, I can smell things, I begin to create my own dialogue, so very much part of the duoethnography graphic nature is the concept of storytelling, so in duoethnography we both express and explain. When I give feedback on papers that's one of the things I point out, not just in courses but in the books that we are co-editing and as a referee for journals. Too much explanation loses that ontological feel and that it is through expression that narratives work. The axiological dimension is that the ontological evokes readers' stories, brings their voices into the virtual trialogue. Today, if we were to name the methodology, I would suggest trioethnography, making the reader's present explicit.

Sean: The boundaries and intersections of *theoria*, *praxis*, and *poiesis* is a way to explain the difference between epistemology and ontology. In the expressive (*poiesis*) we can show how we live our practices (*praxis*), and how we have been living *is welcome* in the classroom where too often *theoria* is privileged and exclusive in school spaces. Students often dichotomize who they are as teachers and who they are outside of the classroom, so I invite them to bring these identities together, to live and represent themselves in the classroom more fully. In my own life, being a poet, I've asked myself what it means to teach poetically. For my students, I help them get beyond epistemology by integrating knowing, doing, and making.

Joe: For me, the act of conducting a duoethnography is a curriculum itself. We learn through its constructions and we reconceptualize ourselves and the world in which we inhabit through the dialogue.

Rick: I also like them to beware of the lived curriculum within the class, so we read Ted Aoki (2005a) and the embodied curriculum. Many of them will want to do a topic that is related to something important to themselves and then they tend to not to want to deconstruct but rather just reify it in some way. So, maybe, what I need to emphasize more is not who they are but who they are becoming.

Joe: And that gets to that notion of "moving towards", Sean.

Sean: I like that phrasing, moving toward. I first encountered it in an academic way in your article *Towards the Use of the "Great Wheel" as a Model in Determining the Quality and Merit of Arts-Based Projects* (Norris, 2011). In my everyday life as a researcher and teacher, even in hallway conversations with colleagues, I have the opportunity to say we don't have to have this all figured out, we can even change our minds and take things in a different direction. Moving toward is about growth, and ironically (given that I am in an education faculty) so many of the dilemmas I encounter in a day are framed as final, or fixed in place, as if everything in our future depends on getting it right, right now.

Something I'd like to emphasize a bit more is how engaging in duoethnography makes the participants a little more aware, and simply having this increased awareness permits more openness to the complexity around them, and then they can be more intentional about noticing who they are, not holding on so tightly to these reified and simplified notions of what and who teachers are supposed to be. What I find troubling is this tendency for new teachers to shape themselves into the social construct of what they perceive teachers to be.

Joe: If I can rephrase that in light of what you just said, Sean. It is not as much who they are, but who they are becoming.

Rick: Maxine Greene's (1973) concept of *Teacher as Stranger* fits in here as she puts the emphasis on choice as we become aware of how we want to change and who we want to be as human beings and in trying to become conscious.

Joe: A while ago I began to play with the terms accept/encourage/reject, and concluded that teaching is a destructive act. We must always reject our students for who they are, and accept them for who they may become. No matter what we do we are expecting students to grow, to change. In a scene in *Great Expectations* (Norris & Mirror Theater, 1994) I play a coach providing feedback, "If you go backwards you might do it a little bit higher." One student may consider that encouragement, another student could consider it a putdown or rejection and a third, acknowledgement of ability. In fact, all three co-exist. So I believe that in every pedagogical act there is an act of rejection. In all learning we reject our present selves as we move toward our future selves. So, Rick, in an example you told me about a student who explored religion, he resisted moving forward, and entrenched himself where he was. He rejected a possible future self. This of course is within his purview. I use the terms stop, start, and continue as a way of making decisions about insights gleaned from any form of reflective practice. A key aspect of duoethnography is an openness to become.

Rick: And it's difficult. With this particular student, he thought that he had encountered a dominant anti-religion narrative which he sought to resist. But he could not interrogate his own position in relation to that understanding. He saw himself as offering a counter-narrative to that larger narrative. But I do think that counter-narratives are important as well—not to close them but to allow duoethnography to give expression to them. So in some ways I was open to his plight as a construction.

Sean: Exactly. Duoethnography is not something that you do to another person, or to yourself for that matter; in the same way, teaching is not something we do to another person. I emphasize this because I've come across too many metaphors that present teaching as an activity that one does to another person, and I would rather understand it as a process of living in the same moment.

Joe: I use the term invite. We invite a person to join us on our quest, to dwell in our quest(ion). We recognize our own inadequacy from Levinas' (1984) perspective, and invite another person to see our construction in a different way. Through their lens we can reconceptualize ourselves; we become (re)knewed(re)known.

Sean: That's beautiful.

Rick: It's hard to live in the moment—to be open to that dynamic text. But to do this is important. I have students who just want the answer, who just want knowledge to be given to them and for things to be definite and certain, as opposed to fluid. And of course this relates to Bhabha's (1991, 1994) concept of the third space that Aoki (2005b) applies into curriculum studies.

Joe: My duoethnography with Olenka Bilash (Norris & Bilash, 2016) addresses student resistance to uncertainty. The hegemony of the "right answer" is heavily engrained. I regard duoethnography as Neo's red pill.

> You take the blue pill, the story ends. You wake up in your bed and believe whatever you want to believe. You take the red pill, you stay in Wonderland, and I show you how deep the rabbit hole goes. (Wachowski & Wachowski, 1999)

It can be an act of self-liberation.

As I look through my notes another issue that arises is the difference in writing a duoethnography for a course and the writing of a duoethnography for publication. While one chapter in this book does both, I think that I underemphasized a sense of audience in my teaching. I still think, to a certain extent, duoenthnographies for courses are written like most papers, for the professor. A fundamental aspect of duoethnography is that it is not only about the writer's learnings, duoethnographers are also trying to create a third space for their readers. If there's one thing I might do a little differently the next time, if given the opportunity to teach duoethnography, is to emphasize that the text should move beyond the partnership with an awareness of a larger audience. Duoethnographies don't merely report; they question. In so doing they evoke responses from their readers.

Rick: Yes, the notion of audience is really important and for people to begin to examine their own work through the eyes of the other and then to try to imagine it in a different way.

Joe: Sean, your thoughts on that?

Sean: What comes to mind is the difference between explaining and interpreting. Sometimes when students are writing for the professor they become overly rhetorical, like they're trying to control the argument, but what I am looking for is their curiosity.

Joe: Strong point, curiosity is an important dimension of duoethnography.

Sean: I want them to let me hear their interpretation unfold, including their doubts and uncertainties. In this way, when I hear the narrator struggle with an idea, the presentation of the evidence has a narrative arc that advances the text in interesting ways. I think duoethnography foregrounds inquiry in such a unique way for students that I can hear their query, I can hear the curiosity better.

Joe: Yes, it is much harder for two people to control a text than one.

Rick: Before we move on can I ask if there are any dilemmas or troubling or difficult things that we've encountered?

Joe: I try to underplay my own expertise. Rick and I are the creators of duoethnography and have generated a set of basic tenets. But there are also a number of colleagues who have helped us to refine the methodology. But hey, Rick's and my names are on the cover. Students are steeped in a curriculum of please the teacher. The challenge is to create spaces where they are comfortable to move way beyond pleasing the teacher into the inquiry, but if you really immerse yourself in the inquiry, ironically, you'll please the teacher.

Sean: A dilemma I face is when writers (and I include myself here) come up against their own worry and anxiety, and to combat these feelings they move into abstraction, a kind of *academicese*, a language that we have all learned at some point in our lives in order to please professorial readers. Deep and sustained reflection that is located in the inner self is very difficult, not only because of the protective layers that we use to insulate ourselves from others, but also because in academic contexts subjectivity is too often marginalized. When writers move into the realm of abstraction, memories, identities, and reflections are kept in the subtext or excluded from the text altogether. But, as a reader, because I want to know a writer's story and her/his storytelling voice, what matters are the details that are unique to who they are. In duoethnography, when the life story is processed and analyzed with another's perspective, and then represented in an aesthetic way, the dilemma of abstraction is avoided. Not always, but certainly that is the hope.

Joe: This is that explain/express balance.

Rick: The abstraction makes it safe as they don't connect themselves to their own stories. I find that it is almost a catharsis with students that they've been socialized into this notion of abstraction and that when they begin to enter their own story, it is often painful but also a release. I had two students do a duoethnography about ways in which they were either identifiers or counter-identifiers toward schooling. And the person who thought that she had always been the good student and then wanted to be the good teacher who taught as her teachers had—she realized that she may have been motivated to be the good teacher as an act of compliance. She recognized an insecurity in her in the past in wanting to accept the status quo. To move from that safe notion she experienced some major dissonance. The notion of self in the classroom can be very complex and difficult.

Joe: And the methodology does ask duoethnographers to disrupt themselves. Like Shiva we need to continually rise from the ashes, and grow as learners. We have to be willing to enter painful situations, and reflection should do that; it is not a romantic notion. How dare we as teachers create spaces of dissonance for students, how dare we not?

Rick: And I think that we model this in our own work; we show ourselves in vulnerable ways, that we are willing to go through that.

Joe: Vulnerability. Rick, we haven't talked about vulnerability yet in our writings, have we? We implied it in discussions about trust, but we haven't really haven't delved deeply into vulnerability.

Sean: I'm more open for students to navigate their vulnerability with one another when they foreground that what they are constructing is an aesthetic piece, whether it's text, or live performance, or something represented graphically. As they build their relationship over the three or four classes, I remind them to make deliberate and conscious choices about what they can share or not share, but also that the aesthetic representation provides another layer or an in-between space for them to explore vulnerability. Emily Dickinson (1951a) is famous for saying, "Tell the truth, but tell it slant."[2]

Joe: I use a public/personal/private continuum to make this distinction. Public is anything anyone can know about you. Private are things that you don't want anyone else to know about, and personal is that space between public and personal. They are things that you don't mind people knowing but don't readily tell or things that are private that in certain contexts you are willing to reveal. The degree of vulnerability is up to each duoethnographer as to what she/he wishes to bring forward into first the personal level when writing the duoethnography and the public level when decisions are made about what to retain and what to discard.

Sean: We become open to another as we release certain stories to them. This is an act of vulnerability. You said this earlier in our conversation, Joe. One of the reasons why I introduce duoethnography at the beginning of the course is I'm trying to warm up the room; the ways students are vulnerable to one another in the duoethnography does that. I want to construct a safe place but I am also very aware that no one can control the safety of a room. While they aren't separate vulnerabilities, I find it helpful to think of an analytical space comprised only of the two people involved in the duoethnography and an aesthetic space when the work is made public. In the analytic space I invite students to be personal to one another, explaining how in this space their lives are data, and there can be a unique vulnerability that emerges between them because their interest in one another often goes beyond their interpretations of the data. Toward the end of the research process, I talk about what it means for knowledge to become public. Their audience to one another is different than the public audience. As they move into the aesthetic space, I invite them to shape the story, turning it into more of an artistic piece. Moving between different spaces takes conscious awareness of what can and cannot be shared, and that is part of learning how to be a teacher.

Joe: Rick and Sean, I direct this question to both of you because I no longer have this experience. An implication here and perhaps a challenge is the field experience. Do either of you go into the field and supervise student teachers?

Sean: I used to, but not for a few years.

Joe: Part of my curiosity is in what you see as the pros and cons of knowing these personal stories as you interact with them in the field. When I was at Washington State University I did go into the field every year, and I'm curious how this could create a warmth of relationship, Sean, that you are talking about. Or, could it also work against it, that is, know that I know your story, when I see you in the field I could use this for or against you.

Sean: My impression is this, and I'm basing my impression on the fact that I am getting out into the field and having conversations with English language arts teachers who are cooperating teachers for our Bachelor of Education students. The trend here locally is depersonalization; a teacher is a teacher is a teacher. One teacher is as good as another. The instrumental and mechanistic approach is deliberate in our district, the rationale being that there is a better overall quality when the classes are more alike from teacher to teacher and school to school. In PEI, for the first time ever, students must now pass a literacy test in order to graduate. With this introduction of high stakes testing the intention is to ensure teachers are covering the curriculum in similar ways and with similar emphases. Curriculum is being conceived narrowly as the plan and being a professional means leaving your private life outside the classroom—teachers' and students' stories of who they are don't matter—so I remind my students that they may not end up teaching in PEI, that in other places in the world they will need to be aware of how other people think about teaching. At the university I try and push against some of what is happening in the district. I prod, and provoke, and push to create conversation around these issues.

Rick: Your question is a good one, Joe—the interplay between duoethnography and who they are or how they react when they enter their own classroom in their preinternship or their internship. We are trying to construct some partnerships right now with schools so that when they enter the classroom they are already working with communities; however, they often focus on the curriculum of the teacher whose classroom that they are in. My preservice students are often sort of critical that it's often a reform-based curriculum and they keep saying that the teacher is missing all these opportunities to enter into the lived world of their students. And so it's difficult because then they enter this closed neoliberal space and it's hard to go beyond that space and consider how to negotiate it and allow the secondary students to express through an emergent lived curriculum.

Sean: A duoethnography between a preservice teacher and a cooperating teacher would unpack some of this, particularly in my PEI context.

Joe: My first book, *Learning to Teach Drama a Case Narrative Approach* (Norris, McCammon, & Miller, 2000), gets at some of that. Each chapter starts with a student-written case narrative about a particular issue. It is followed by a response written by a student from a subsequent year to provide an experience-far perspective. It also includes responses from cooperating teachers. Though the exchange is not conversational multiple perspectives are given.

Sean: What I would find interesting would be the different power dynamics.

Rick: It would be interesting … you could have the students select a topic and maybe they could explore it together in pairs—preservice teacher/preservice teacher—and then after that take it out to the field and have it be preservice/in-service teacher and have them look at the same topic. Just understanding the difference and gaining a greater sort of meta-view of the system and the interplay between what we do at the university and what is actually happening in the field. Then for us to actually research that through this methodology and to allow our students to deconstruct it and to have some agency over that would be very interesting.

Joe: Exactly. Bringing it back to our students and have them write responses to it as well.

Rick: Right.

Joe: So, I think we've changed the title of our chapter. It was originally titled "teaching duoethnography in graduate curriculum theory courses", which we could semi-change to "teaching duoethnography in curriculum theory and teacher education courses", or now I'm thinking it could even be "Living curriculum theory through duoethnography".

Let's turn to assessment for a moment. Rick and I have given feedback to colleagues and also grade students' assignments that were written as duoethnographies. The expository essay has been the assessment staple for decades. It's been hegemonic and so overdone, but it's comfortable because it's so well-known. When reading duoethnographies, I cannot respond in the same way. For example, "There could be more expression", "You have more theoretical than analytical", "There are opportunities to integrate the literature", and so on. I thought we could problematize the criteria/tenets of duoethnography. What are the types of responses that you find yourself giving to students?

Rick: I have issues with assessment in general. And with duoethnography I think that there is a range in the quality of their work in general in terms of praxis or change, but I don't think that it has to happen immediately. Duoethnography never really ends: it continues to resonate in different ways. Even people who reify their views may change these views in the future. And when you reify your views, maybe you are starting to challenge them on some level. So I have a hard time with assessment. But I do emphasize if there are some people who have written something that is really excellent, I'll keep emphasizing those good examples in class.

Sean: I'm in the same camp, Rick. I abhor putting numbers on things and fortunately for me I'm in a program that is pass/fail. While our faculty likes to say that a pass means 80 %, I don't actually like to convert student work to a percentage-based scale. I find that if students are committed to the process, if they are able to enter into a space where they can articulate reality differently, then I feel that that is a fair contribution. The only other thing I might be looking for is their sense of reflexivity, so that they have offered something significant in the way that they express their work.

Rick: How about you, Joe?

Joe: I guess that we all went to the same camp. When I taught at Mount St. Vincent University in their summer institutes, some instructors would say everyone gets an A until you prove differently. I followed that practice. So I, too, find giving greater numbers very difficult. Now for the student paper that is going into this book my first set of responses were based upon the qualities for the course. Now I was much more demanding in relation to qualities for a published piece because there is an audience with a different set of expectations.

Mathematics educators Zack and Reid (2003) employ Varela's, Thompson's, and Rosch's (1993) perspective on "good-enough". If education is about growth then each act is a stepping stone to the next. Mackey (1997) calls these "placeholders" (p. 440). I look at the potential, the moving toward that elusive understanding, that you discuss, Sean. A willingness to dwell in the question, an openness to uncertainty, a resistance to closure and getting it right are some of the tones of duoethnographies. I also provide comments about the balance of express and explain, a sense that there is real listening to another, and that a learning/transformation is explicit in the way that the duoethnography is written, so there is evidence of learning.

Rick: Reflexivity is really important. And there was one article that I can think of where two people selected each other to just basically reinforce each other's views and they just ended up constructing a polemic. So for me it's important that you are open to the views of the other. One of the biggest problems humanity is facing right now with this era of increasing globalization is learning from difference in a way that doesn't reinforce universalism. Wang (2006) offers this thought about third space theory that I think can be applied to duoethnography:

> [In] a third space … both parts of a conflicting (cultural, gendered, classed, national or psychic) double interact with and transform each other so that multiplicity of the self gives rise to a new realm of subjectivity in new areas of negotiation. (120–121)

It is this multiplicity of the self in relation to a different Other that animates duoethnography.

All: This chapter has reinforced for us that we don't merely teach duoethnography; rather, duoethnography is imbedded in much larger discourses of teacher identity and the purpose of education. As we conversed, we elicited nuances that connected to theories that have underpinned our work.

Notes

1. In Canada, the Bachelor of Education degree is typically a two-year after-degree program that best corresponds to a Masters of Teaching in the United States, not their Bachelor of Education degree.

2. Tell all the Truth but tell it slant.
   Success in Circuit lies
   Too bright for our infirm Delight
   The Truth's superb surprise
   As Lightning to the Children eased
   With explanation kind
   The Truth must dazzle gradually
   Or every man be blind—
   Emily Dickinson (1951b)

References

Aoki, T. (2005a). Toward understanding "computer application" (1987/1999). In W. Pinar & R. Irwin (Eds.), *Toward curriculum inquiry in a new key: The collect works of Ted T. Aoki* (pp. 151–158). Mahwah: Lawrence Erlbaum Associates, Publishers.

Aoki, T. (2005b). Locating living pedagogy in teacher "research": Five metonymic moments (2003). In W. Pinar & R. Irwin (Eds.), *Toward curriculum inquiry in a new key: The collect works of Ted T. Aoki* (pp. 425–432). Mahwah: Lawrence Erlbaum Associates, Publishers.

Aoki, T. T., Pinar, W., & Irwin, R. L. (2005). *Curriculum in a new key: The collected works of Ted T. Aoki.* Mahwah, NJ: Lawrence Erlbaum Associates, Publishers.

Barone, T. E. (1990). Using the narrative text as an occasion for conspiracy. In E. W. Eisner & A. Peshkin (Eds.), *Qualitative inquiry in education* (pp. 305–326). New York: Teachers College Press.

Bhabha, H. K. (1991). The third space. In J. Rutherford (Ed.), *Identity: Community, culture, difference.* London, UK: Lawrence and Wishart.

Bhabha, H. K. (1994). *The location of culture.* New York, NY: Routledge.

Bochner, A. P., & Ellis, C. (2002). *Ethnographically speaking: Autoethnography, literature, and aesthetics.* Walnut Creek: AltaMira Press.

Britzman, D. (2009). The poetics of supervision: A psychoanalytic experiment for teacher education. *Changing English, 16*(4), 385–396.

Britzman, D. P. (1998). *Lost subjects, contested objects: Toward a psychoanalytic inquiry of learning.* Albany, NY: State University of New York Press.

Chambers, C., Hasebe-Ludt, E., Leggo, C., & Sinner, A. (2012). *A heart of wisdom: Life writing as empathetic inquiry.* New York: Peter Lang Publishers.

Clandinin, D. J., & Connelly, F. M. (1995). *Teachers' professional knowledge landscape.* New York: TC Press.

Clandinin, D. J., & Connelly, F. M. (2000). *Narrative inquiry: Experience and story in qualitative research.* San Francisco: Jossey-Bass Publishers.

Clandinin, J. D., & Connelly, F. M. (1988). The idea of curriculum. In J. Clandinin & M. Connelly (Eds.), *Teachers as curriculum planners*. New York: Teachers College Press.

Clandinin, J. D., & Connelly, F. M. (1992). Teacher as curriculum maker. In P. W. Jackson (Ed.), *Handbook of research in curriculum* (pp. 402–435). New York: Macmillan.

Costner, K. (Writer). (1990). *Dances with wolves*. Los Angeles, CA: Orion Pictures.

de Freitas, E., & McAuley, A. (2008). Teaching for diversity by troubling whiteness: Strategies for classrooms in isolated white communities. *Race Ethnicity and Education, 11*(4), 429–442. doi:10.1080/13613320802479018.

Dickinson, E. (1951a). *The poems of Emily Dickinson* (R. Franklin, Ed.). Cambridge, MA: Harvard University Press.

Dickinson, E. (1951b). Tell all the truth but tell it slant. Retrieved from http://www.poetryfoundation.org/poems-and-poets/poems/detail/56824

Freire, P. (1986). *Pedagogy of the oppressed*. New York: The Continuum Publishing Corporation.

Gadamer, H. (1975). *Truth and method*. New York: Crossroad.

Gardner, H. (1993). *Frames of mind*. New York: Basic Books.

Geertz, C. (1974). From the native's point of view: On the nature of anthropological understanding. In P. Rabinow & W. Sullivan (Eds.), *Interpretive social sciences* (pp. 221–237). Berkeley: University of California Press.

Greene, M. (1973). *Teacher as stranger: Educational philosophy for the modern age*. Belmont, CA: Wadsworth Publishing.

Henderson, J. (1992). *Reflective teaching: Becoming an inquiring educator*. Toronto: Maxwell Macmillan Canada.

Lévinas, E. (1984). Emmanuel Lévinas. In R. Kearney (Ed.), *Dialogues with contemporary continental thinkers* (pp. 47–70). Manchester: Manchester University Press.

Lortie, D. (1975). *Schoolteacher: A sociological study*. Chicago: University of Chicago Press.

MacDonald, B. J. (1995). *Theory as a prayerful act: The collected essays of James B. MacDonald*. New York: Peter Lang.

Mackey, M. (1997). Good-enough reading: Momentum and accuracy in the reading of complex fiction. *Research in the Teaching of English, 31*(4), 428–458.

McLeod, J. (1987). The arts and education. In J. Simpson (Ed.), *Education and the arts*. Edmonton, Alberta: Fine Arts Council, Alberta Teachers' Association.

McLuhan, M. (1964). *Understanding media: The extensions of man*. New York: McGraw-Hill.

Norris, J. (2008). A quest for a theory and practice of authentic assessment: An arts based approach. *LEARNing Landscapes, 2*(1), 211–233.

Norris, J. (2009). *Playbuilding as qualitative research: A participatory arts-based approach*. Walnut Creek: Left Coast Press.

Norris, J. (2011). Towards the use of the 'Great Wheel' as a model in determining the quality and merit of arts-based projects (research and instruction). *International Journal of Education & the Arts, 12* (Arts & Learning Research Journal Special Issue: Selected Papers from the 2010 AERA Arts & Learning SIG), 1–24 Retrieved from http://www.ijea.org/v12si1/index.html.

Norris, J., & Bilash, O. (2016). A journey towards mutualist teaching and learning: A collaborative reflective practice on community building and democratic classrooms. In R. D. Sawyer & J. Norris (Eds.), *Interdisciplinary reflective practice through duoethnography: Examples for educators.* New York: Palgrave Macmillan.

Norris, J., & Mirror Theatre. (1994). (Director, Actor and co-author with student company). *Great expectations.* Edmonton: Instructional Technology Center, University of Alberta.

Norris, J., McCammon, L., & Miller, C. (2000). *Learning to teach drama: A case narrative approach.* Portsmouth: Heinemann.

Nussbaum, M. (2009). Education for profit, education for freedom. *Liberal Education,* Summer, 6–39.

Pinar, W. (1981). The reconceptualization of curriculum studies. In H. Giroux, A. Penna, & W. Pinar (Eds.), *Curriculum and instruction.* Berkeley: McCutchan Publishing Corporation.

Pinar, W. (1994). The method of Currere (1975). In W. Pinar (Ed.), *Autobiography, politics and sexuality: Essays in curriculum theory 1972–1992* (pp. 19–27). New York: Peter Lang.

Ramis, H. (Director). (1993). *Groundhog Day.* Culver City: Columbia Pictures.

Rankie Shelton, N., & McDermott, M. (2011). A curriculum of beauty. In J. Norris, R. D. Sawyer, & D. Lund (Eds.), *Duoethnography: Dialogic methods for social, health, and educational research.* New York: Routledge.

Reason, P., & Hawkins, P. (1988). Storytelling as inquiry. In P. Reason (Ed.), *Human inquiry in action* (pp. 79–101). Newbury Park: Sage Publications.

Rosenblatt, L. (1978). *The reader, the text, the poem: The transactional theory of the literary work.* Carbondale, IL: Southern Illinois Press.

Sawyer, R., & Norris, J. (2015). Hidden and null curricula of sexual orientation: A duoethnography of the absent presence and the present absence. *International Review of Qualitative Research, 8*(1), 5–26.

Scudder, J. J. (1968). Freedom with authority: A Buber model for teaching. *Educational Theory, 18*(Spring), 133–142.

Smith, J., & Heshusius, L. (1986). Closing down the conversation: The end of the quantitative-qualitative debate among educational inquirers. *Educational Researcher, 15*(1), 4–12. doi:10.3102/0013189x015001004.

Varela, F., Thompson, E., & Rosch, E. (1993). *The embodied mind: Cognitive science and human experience.* Cambridge: MIT Press.

Wachowski, A., & Wachowski, L. (Directors). (1999). *The Matrix*. Burbank, CA: Warner Brothers.

Wang, C. C., & Burris, M. A. (1997). Photovoice: Concept, methodology, and use for participatory needs assessment. *Health Education & Behavior, 24*, 369–387.

Wang, H. (2006). Speaking as an alien: Is a curriculum in a third space possible? *Journal of Curriculum Theorizing, 22*(1), 111–126.

Weizenbaum, J. (1984). Limits in the use of computer technology: Need for a Man-centered science. In D. Sloan (Ed.), *Toward the recovery of wholeness: Knowledge, education, and human values* (pp. 149–158). New York: Teachers College Press.

Wiebe, S., Sameshima, P., Irwin, R., Leggo, C., Gouzouasis, P., & Grauer, K. (2007). Re-imagining arts integration: Rhizomatic relations of the everyday. *Journal of Educational Thought, 41*(3), 263–280.

Zack, V., & Reid, D. A. (2003). Good-enough understanding: Theorising about the learning of complex ideas (Part 1). *For the Learning of Mathematics, 23*(3), 43–50.

Zwick, E. (Writer). (2003). *The Last Samurai*. Santa Clarita: Warner Bros.

CHAPTER 3

Right and Wrong (and Good Enough): A Duoethnography within a Graduate Curriculum Studies Course

Nat Banting and Stéphan De Loof

Prologue

Educational stakeholders are familiar with the idea of a "subject". The explicit curriculum (Eisner, 1985) is divided into academic domains each with their specific areas of inquiry. It enables educational institutions at every level to create programs of study by choosing pieces from various subjects—a sort of educational alchemy. Flinders, Noddings, and Thornton (1986) describe the typical explicit curriculum as one that consists of "mathematics, science, social studies, English, art, and physical education" (p. 34). Such an ordering is typical of the power hierarchy created between content areas in schools. This remnant of our modern enlightenment toward rationalism, certainty, and industrialization places disciplines perceived to contain academic rigor above those perceived as vocational and employable. This rationalism is bolstered by an objectivism that underpins the activities of the mathematical and scientific. Here, school upholds the abstraction of the individual as the ultimate goal of scientific pursuit. The result is a certainty in outcomes that uses the

N. Banting (✉) • S. De Loof
University of Alberta, Edmonton, AB, Canada

J. Norris, *Theorizing Curriculum Studies, Teacher Education, and Research through Duoethnographic Pedagogy*,
DOI 10.1057/978-1-137-51745-6_3

dichotomy of right and wrong to describe the world. The core curriculum establishes itself on the basis of right and wrong, the existence of this perfection, and its non-interpretive (objective) nature.

In an educational milieu that is calling for stakeholders to validate the culture in which the learner resides as more than an impotent social construct, teachers need to question the assumptions that lie beneath the hegemony of the core subjects. The curriculum of the core is often explicitly stated in the form of graduation requirements, postsecondary entrance requirements, and standardized examinations, but is perpetuated through implicit undertones of intellectualism and rigor. It manifests itself through compulsory courses, topic inclusion in wide-scale testing, and political attention over raising standards (Robinson, 2001).

Using a duoethnographic methodology (Norris & Sawyer, 2012), the perspectives of two teachers in the midst of graduate studies coemerge (Kieren & Simmt, 2009) with regard to the power and prestige structures set up by the notion of the hidden curriculum of *right*. Nat is a secondary mathematics teacher in Saskatoon, Saskatchewan, and Stéphan is a secondary career and technology teacher currently teaching welding and woodworking in Calgary, Alberta. At the time of this writing, Stéphan was two courses shy of completing his Master's degree, and Nat was two courses into his program. Their impressions of, and interactions with, the idea of *right* unfold, shift, and co-implicate as they share experiences as students and teachers. By examining and accepting differing perspectives, they are able to *try on* another point of view, enrich the imagination of the alternate lens, and expand their understanding of the issue (Mezirow, 2000). As the experiences are presented, they are reexamined, enlightened by literature, and reconceptualized by the authors as their lenses enter a more enlightened space.

The full transformative nature of the piece cannot be experienced without seeing how conversations opened up avenues of interpretations previously closed in a monologic sense. The process of interweaving dialogues into a coherent yet dissonant whole was one of many edits and revisions. To include every shift would be far beyond the scope of this chapter, but we hope the coalescence can be read through the text. The process is not meant to conclude with an omnipotent lens, but, in a similar vein to Krammer and Mangiardi (2012), the reader is invited to enter the conversation, contrast their own experiences within the narratives, and welcome new insights that the duoethnographic process affords. A foundation of reminiscence on their respective backgrounds situates the two voices as they focus conversations around questions regarding their experience with *right* throughout their lives. Best attempts were made to define central questions that seemed to form through the dialogue; these questions are used as headings throughout the chapter, but do not represent the duoethnographic process. In reality, this is a highly streamlined account of a convoluted process.

Impressions of Duoethnography as a Graduate Assignment

Stéphan: When I first started this project, I was nervous knowing that I would have to enlarge my boundaries in order to present a worthy project. At the same time it gave me a chance to get out of my comfort zone, go beyond my perceived limitations, and reflect on my past. How can I give new meaning to past experience? How to begin the dialogue with myself? What is the true power of reflexivity?

Nat: I had a plan in my mind that detailed how this course was going to go. I emailed ahead for the readings, completed many of them, and began brainstorming ideas for the major assignments. I was well aware that arts-based assessment (Norris, 2008) was encouraged, and this scared me. My art (mathematics) is often perceived as rigid and driven even when it is employed expressively.

There is that awkward tension that exists around the table on the morning of the first day of a graduate class (of any course, really). You, Stéphan, busied yourself preparing your materials. I opted to bring a laptop and pretended to be enthralled in the latest research article or interesting tidbit of educational drawl that just scrolled across my social media timeline. That is just like me. I am constantly consuming—organizing a worldview. As you did your best to seem busy, others did the same. Some prepared notebooks with headings and others switched phones to vibrate. We did anything to remain inconspicuous. I had no idea that I would become so open with Stéphan throughout this course through this vehicle of duoethnography. At the beginning, he was just another student playing the same game I was. When Stéphan proposed the idea of duoethnography, I took on the challenge because I enjoyed the ease with which I entered into dialogue with a duoethnographic piece in the course readings (Norris & Sawyer, 2004). I also enjoyed the perspectives that Stéphan had brought to initial class discussions. He was bold and straightforward, and—aside from poor taste in sporting allegiances—exemplified the wisdom of a seasoned teacher. In short, he was *good enough*. (A running theme to become evident as this chapter unfolds.)

If I were being honest, duoethnography also seemed simple to me. Tell some stories, find common ground, make a concession or two, and move on. I learned many things through this process. Most importantly, there is a huge difference between monologues emerging concurrently and dialogues coemerging.

Stéphan: The other difficult part was to put complete trust in someone else, in this case Nat. Not only did I not know him before this class started, but he is a math teacher and I am a shop teacher. We are so different physically and mentally; he is tall and lanky, and I am shorter and stockier. We are wired differently in many ways. He is the smart one that acts upon analysis and uses big words, big names, and citations. (I would like to use the phrase *brilliant mind*, but I don't want it to go to his head.) On the contrary, I act upon gut instinct, use simple words with fuzzy citations, and only sometimes get the right author's name for them. These tensions made for a great relationship. A colleague in our class used the analogy of a clothespin in one of his arts-based assignments (Norris, 2008), and it fits perfectly here. As tension is applied to one end, it provides an opening, a catalyst for movement at the other. In order to move toward transformation, you need to live at a point of tension. It is the only way that the process can fulfill its purpose.

Nat: Unlike Stéphan, my main difficulty was an internal one. I had a very hard time looking for introspective sources of knowledge. I wanted to complete the process correctly without ever knowing what correct looked like. In hindsight, my analytic structure was doomed from the start because the cognitive distress caused by another opinion created a moving target. I kept suggesting possible headings and topics to scaffold our work, but they always seemed to become irrelevant after conversations. The process required a weaving not only of stories, perceptions, and worldviews, but of styles and preferences. The frustrating thing for me was the fact that duoethnography ensures that you are never reading or writing the complete story (Zack & Reid, 2003). The collective knowledge space is built through our interactions (Kieren & Simmt, 2009). The following account is a snapshot that needed to be penned on a deadline. It attempts to provide a notion of co-implication, but cannot be considered complete. This is incredibly frustrating for me—as is evidenced throughout this piece.

Stéphan: We have to celebrate difference with all teachers; it is important to remind ourselves that we are not teaching to get a pat on the back or to have people comment on how great we are. Our first goal is to help students realize their full potential, or at least give them the tools to realize it. I truly believe students need to have a wide array of teachers so they come in contact with a full spectrum of personalities, teaching methods, and strategies in order for them to reach that goal. The *eureka* in education comes from variety and the hope that something will strike a chord with the learners.

Nat: Stéphan and I continually arrived at the fact that we are both teachers, and that provides common ground for our conversations. We both have the best interests of students in mind, and we both want, above all, success for these students. Upon further conversation, we (rather expectedly) confirmed that our paths to the profession and ideas of success rooted in our respective subject areas looked very different.

Our Upbringings and Their Effect on Our View of *Right*

Stéphan: I was raised in a small town outside of Montréal. I come from a family where my mother was the youngest of seven kids, but the first one to finish high school. My dad lived through World War II, and it is still unclear if he finished grade six. Nonetheless, education was a really important part of our upbringing. I still hear my dad—now 85—saying that none of his kids will earn a living breaking their backs like he had to. He likes to show the black and white pictures of him (in post-war Belgium) plowing a field with two horses. He explains how hard it is to plow a field with one beast, and then asks us to imagine two. He always says that a better education would have kept him from plowing so many fields. The reality is, to this day, I still love working hard and sacrificing my body to give a break to my mind. He made sure that we realized the sacrifices he had to make so we all had the opportunity to go to school.

Nat: I was raised as one of four children of two educated parents. Both my mother and father taught at a local college when I was growing up in Prince Edward Island. They both grew up on small town farms in Saskatchewan, and my siblings and I knew that education was important. My father is a voracious reader and eloquent communicator.

Stéphan: Crazy, my dad used to read the newspaper, but I do not think I saw him read a book until he was about 50 years old. (It was about fly fishing—a passion of his.)

Nat: It would be hard to think of a time where dad wasn't reading a book (or at least wishing he was). I never appreciated my mother as an academic until I was old enough to understand her past. She gave up further educational opportunities to raise her family; this is something I am beginning to respect more as my young son adds to the time pressure of work and school life. Weekly readings are now interrupted by repeated performances of *The Very Hungry Caterpillar* and only bedtime provides enough uninterrupted time to work on term papers.

It's interesting how every person thinks their experience is typical until it is contrasted with that of others. I could not unpack my own upbringing until Stéphan provided his. I have always craved stability, and believed that stability comes through hard work. Maybe that is why a subject like mathematics, often validated on the grounds of "academic rationalism" (Eisner, 1985), called me. I always valued my education above all else. To me, the accumulation of knowledge was the key to future stability.

Stéphan: Was my formal education that important for me? I don't think so. I did well in school; with my marks I could have gone to any college I wanted. All my years of traveling delayed my settling down and was the true foundation of my education. I left home at 16 to go to college, and learn to live on my own. I finished my first degree and got a great job by 20, but was way too young to settle into a routine. I still remember my parents' expression when I told them I was quitting my cushy government job in the genetic department of Agriculture Canada to go work doing pipeline construction as a welder's helper in Northern Alberta. They thought I was crazy; looking back, I was just looking for more (and I got it). It was the start of a seven-year hiatus where I would work hard from September to May, then go back home to work in the agricultural field and enjoy the summers with family and friends. I never struck it rich, but I did learn that you don't judge a man by his marks but by his values and the way he treats others.

Nat: I worked hard in school because it was important. My grandfather told many stories about homesteading in southern Saskatchewan and my outlook was very much one of meritocracy. This meshed perfectly with the linear accumulation of knowledge school mathematics provided. If I worked hard, I could master the *hardest* subjects. I did not find the same guarantee in the optional subjects; in a way, the bursts of creativity they necessitated went against my values of consistency and security. What drew me to teaching were the experiences helping others achieve a similar satisfaction of dominance. I loved listening to their conceptualizations on a method, and altering them to synchronize with an ideal procedure. I thought the process was emancipatory, and, with a proper dose of hard work, predictable.

Stéphan: Unlike my dad, I never thought that working with my hands was that bad. All those years when I was traveling, I used a mix of my physical and mental skills to keep going. I milked cows and built concrete foundations; I was able to combine my physical skills and knowledge to land a great job teaching career technology studies. It was those experiences that truly shaped my philosophy of education.

Nat: I underwent a much more traditional formation of my philosophy of education. I knew that if I could understand the theory of education and work hard to prepare myself for classroom situations, it would result in opportunities to provide meaningful mathematical encounters with my students. A strong foundation in mathematics content, preparation in educational theory, and diligent preparation toward practice would ensure success. I have always considered myself a creative teacher, but still operated from a well-prepared space. I gave up lesson planning in favor of lesson preparing very early in my career. Predetermining student actions and key questions was far too rigid. Instead, I learned to anticipate student action, scaffold their thinking, and network within the classroom (Smith & Stein, 2011). Although the pedagogy is emerging in the moment, my actions in the classroom are purposeful. In this way, my upbringing had a profound influence on my development as a teacher and the choice of subject areas.

Paths to the Profession

Stéphan: It is important to mention that I had many lives before becoming a teacher ranging from farm worker, ski bum, construction worker, and the Canadian Armed Forces. Lifestyle, the desire to interact with students, the opportunity to make a difference in students' lives, and the ability to travel were all important factors that made me decide that I wanted to be a teacher. I was in the Armed Forces for three years prior to going back to school to do a degree in education. The first year was exciting. I flew in fighter jets and jumped out of airplanes, but it became repetitive and drab very quickly. During these years I lived at bases in Chilliwack, Cold Lake, Edmonton, and North Bay. I also observed that these conditions were not the ideal environments to raise a family. A lot of personnel were leaving wives and kids behind while deployed for six-month tours in various places in the world—Bosnia, Iraq, and Rwanda. It made me realize family was always to be number one on my agenda.

Nat: I went to university with a clear plan in mind. I had known for a couple years that I wanted to become a teacher. I was afforded plenty of teaching experiences in high school (or so I thought) because people would come to me to get explanations for mathematical concepts. I didn't approach the mathematics any differently than before, but had an engaging personality and a lot of patience. I was not an overly patient man outside of this setting, but mathematics was my comfort zone. I liked that something I found so simple, so linear, was seen as incredibly difficult by so many. It provided me a status. The unmistakable aura of rightness surrounded mathematics. It carried with it a burden of exactness—of orchestrated precision—that made it difficult to master. I was able to synchronize myself to its requirements; it seemed to take place outside of the user, and this placed it at the core of academic pursuit.

Stéphan: I started to reflect about the type of work that would provide me with a lifestyle that would give me the chance to have a lot of time with my family. Based on my so-called talents and affinities, a few options came to mind including fireman, policeman, and teacher. I finally picked teacher because I did not feel that I would like to deal with the negativity that comes with the other two professions. I didn't see myself knocking at a door telling someone that a loved one died in a car accident. The other reason that made me become a teacher was the possibility of traveling. I was lucky enough to be bilingual and it opened a lot of doors. I felt that if I picked the right subjects I could properly tool myself to be able to teach anywhere in Canada or abroad. Lastly, I felt that teaching was a profession that gives you the chance to reinvent yourself. I had found that in previous jobs, such a possibility was hardly there.

Nat: I never thought my motives were based outside an academic interest. Teaching provided an interesting balance between the vocational and theoretical. That is a tension I live between to this day. On the one hand, you are required to communicate like a teenager, but, on the other, you are required to navigate professional channels and base actions in theory. It was a profession where I could use my skills to communicate mathematics. I considered this a valued commodity due to the high number of people I knew who had terrible experiences with math. I also have always enjoyed the process of learning and interacting with young adults. I didn't have the extensive life experience of Stéphan, but now see how the notion of security also played into my decision. Teaching is something I knew and loved. Both my parents taught at the postsecondary level when I was growing up. I have uncles and aunts in the profession. School was safe. While I never had the immediate concerns of raising a family, I knew that teaching wouldn't disrupt this possibility.

While my path and background seemed to reflect the elements that cement math as a core subject—stability, purposiveness, linearity—Stéphan settled on teaching as a best fit to his developed talents. Underlying both decisions was an inherent compatibility, a compatibility rooted in present skills and desires, but also in respective histories—teaching fit.

Interlude

At this point, we shift gears into the precipitates from the discussions. Both of us agreed that detailing our own histories helped situate us in an honest self-evaluation. The discussions that follow recursively situate ourselves back into our personal histories. In doing so, they also create new conversations and add new stories. We made the attempt to organize our discussions into three emergent themes—perfection, creativity and rigor, and intelligence. What follows is a distilled account of our interactions.

Does Perfection Exist and What Does It Look Like?

Nat: I excelled in all subjects in school, but approached them all in a systematic, mathematical way. The idea of certainty—of tidiness—drew me to mathematics. I can remember the chart on the classroom wall. It was off to the left and slightly above my natural field of vision as a fifth grader. Just enough that you could recognize which students were looking at it, trying to figure out their position. This was the weekly tally of the mad minutes, simple multiplication tables we did each day for exactly one minute. The aggregate winner after the week was rewarded with tokens to buy milk at lunch. The best thing about the competition was there was no disputing the winner.

Stéphan: Becoming a teacher was not in the plans early in my life. It is surprising to see where this life has taken me so far. The fact that I am a teacher could almost be considered karma. Growing up, I was probably the worst nightmare a teacher could have in their classroom. I always did well grade-wise, but I was a troublemaker—school was easy for me. I was constantly looking for ways to beat the system. Looking back, I realize that going to school was just a rite of passage; I wanted to travel and see the world. I was building my life so I would have enough tools to reach these goals.

Nat: I enjoyed classes in the practical and applied arts, and still enjoy home improvement projects to this day. Like everything in school, I took it very seriously. I worked hard to achieve a level of precision in all my projects. I approached each project like I would have approached any problem set before me—mathematically. One in particular haunts me to this day, because it is still displayed in my mother's small flower garden. Every visit reminds me of the experience. It is a simple cement stepping stone decorated with colored glass. The pattern is of a single rose against a landscape of blue and green glass (my attempt at a sky and ground). If you were to look at the piece in its finished state, you would have no idea that meticulous time was spent breaking glass pieces until they worked exactly to my liking. Breaking the glass with clumsy hand tools did not allow much room for perfection, but that is what I wanted to achieve. I was helpless and frustrated. In the end, it now sits on the step of my childhood home in its blatant imperfection. A symbol of my artistic ignorance. To make matters worse, my mom purchased another cement stone for the garden. The comparison only accentuates the imperfections.

I felt the same helplessness when I was asked to teach grade nine English during my first year of teaching. (I have exclusively taught mathematics ever since). I remember pouring over student essays wondering how I was to evaluate such personal things like tone, voice, and imagination. The process seemed so foreign and uncomfortable to me.

Stéphan: Unlike Nat's, my experience as a teacher is diverse. I have taught numerous subjects in various school locations. I have taught what the majority would define as core subjects in mathematics and science, fringe subjects of religion and Career and Life Management, and the hands-on options of woodworking, welding, mechanics, and electronics. I know this broad experience provides me with a holistic approach and perspective about the experience of a secondary teacher. I can navigate the different layers involved in teaching various subjects. I use mathematical examples (Yes, Nat, I can do math) with students when welding. Embedding the use of trigonometry, for example, into the drafting of staircases layers multiple disciplines. It is always funny when grade ten students—usually completing the *dash three* trades-oriented math (Alberta Education, 2008)—realize that they have been using trig without knowing it. I feel the many experiences I've had in education give me a wide lens looking at the student's perspective while dealing with the reality of everyday teaching.

Courses like welding or mechanics use a multilayered approach to learning. It is a bricolage of many learning styles. They involve hands-on and hands-off experiences; they are a combination of history, theory, and methods. I have the chance to teach a subject where communication with sounds, words, images, numbers, and gestures comes naturally (McLeod, 1987) in a milieu that favors an I–Thou relationship with the students (Scudder Jr., 1968). I share my experience with the students, and, in return, they add to them. Because we have a common goal in the form of a project, I am able to share a tangible part of their reality. The subject opens common ground where we can initiate a true relationship. The content creates the space for this connection, and if we can cultivate an I–Thou relationship, we minimize the tension that can exist between students and teachers. Teaching in the options values this apprenticeship model. I feel it brings the relationship to the level of mentor as opposed to pupils. Such relationships are not focused on perfection. They provide the students with the tools to move toward self-realization physically, socially, and spiritually.

The best example of that is when you relate your life experience through stories. The usual teacher-storyteller will tell stories of his life successes. Through the years, I realized that the students were way more attentive to my screw-up stories than my successes (probably because they get tired of listening to their parents telling what to do to be perfect). I always share two ironic stories with them about when I was about their age living in Québec. At one point, my dad wanted me to learn how to weld so he would not need to always stop what he was doing when something need to get fixed. I said to him that I did not need to learn how to weld, because I would never use it in my life. Around the same time, I had an argument with my English teacher while trying to explain how stupid it was to learn English in Québec. Why practice something I would never use? I always follow these two stories by telling the students to look at me now; I must be a clown. I teach welding in English. We usually have a good laugh, but it illustrates how important it is to be open to learning because you never know where life will take you. We empower students by having a positive attitude and showing mutual respect; we are creating an awakening. Fundamentally, it should be the school's interest to promote this I–Thou relation at all levels and in all subjects. If this is our focus, perfection takes a back seat. The content shifts around from pupil to pupil, and so ideas of perfection cannot converge at a single point.

Nat: In school, I always had great relationships with my math teachers, but a narrow-sighted view of perfection in the form of correct answers meant that mathematics became cold and austere. I felt that the classroom environment was focused around survival. The focus didn't seem to be on the relationship between the teacher and students (I–Thou or otherwise); the focus was on my relationship with the mathematics. There was a distinct power struggle set up. It was the students on one side and the mathematics on the other. The teacher moved from side to side, sometimes viewed as a lifeline and other times as a public enemy. It was as though the teacher stood as an inhuman communicator of mathematical truth. The student's relationship to the subject matter was more important than the relationship with the teacher. I have always been a very independent person, so I excelled in courses like mathematics where I could wean out the teacher and become my own arbiter of truths. This was easier in math class than the courses you (Stéphan) excelled in. In grade 11, my math teacher would give us handouts with definitions, blanks to fill in, and practice questions. I judged my success that day by how quickly I was able to race ahead of the lecture and understand the day's complexities. Math contained harmless notations that acted in predictable ways. The wood shop was unpredictable. I loved solving problems the industrial arts posed, but hated that I needed to rely so much on the teacher.

Number Theory changed my perspective of mathematics. Most students dreaded the class, but I enjoyed learning the ways in which the numbers seamlessly danced together. It was as though the numbers were interacting, and the mathematicians were just following along picking up on patterns and naming peculiar behavior. The perfection suddenly extended beyond trial and error. Mathematics was able to work with numbers I'd never fathomed, and make sensible claims about them. Through this perfect intricacy, the mathematics was finally in charge in a shocking reversal of roles. In other classrooms, the mathematician was the master and the subject acted as a sort of weapon. Here, the mathematics itself was in control and the student needed to wait patiently, watch—listen. For the first time, mathematics became an open avenue that could be explored. Methods for solution were presented (still in a very restricted sense), but I gained a deep understanding of the topics because I played with them. I would tweak attributes and compare results. As I played with the questions, their meaning deepened, but I also changed alongside them (Proulx & Simmt, 2013). In the classroom, initial conceptions of learners serve as road markers. Students bring me unfinished and haphazard mathematical projects, and we work hard together to bring them toward a perfect, meaningful synthesis. In this way, I see mathematics as very similar to welding, but with a fundamental difference to Stéphan: in mathematics, there is a constant goal of perfection. Getting there is often messy (messiness tells you the solution was worthwhile), but in the end there is answer. So while my tidiness was an illusion, the perfection remains.

Stéphan: First, let's be honest, perfection as an absolute does not exist. Rather than looking toward perfection, I like to think of the philosophy of *good enough*. I believe that every great thing takes hold through an open attitude of *good enough*. Leaving space for improvement baits the hook. This way the learner is not constantly burdened by perfection, but can reflect on improvements and move toward that goal. The "opting for a temporary decision which is good enough for the time being is not only a good move, it is one which we make all the time when in the midst of learning" (Zack & Reid, 2003, p. 43). When one discovers and gets a good grasp of who they are physically, socially, and intellectually they can begin to move closer toward *perfection*.

This idea of *good enough* is best explained with an analogy.

A person goes home one day and their partner asks if they could build them a deck. That person has never built a deck before, but finds all the necessary tools and information to complete construction. When the deck was finished, it looked okay. It was safe, solid, and performing its purpose. It might not have been perfect, but it was *good enough*. After seeing the deck for the first time, the father of that same person asked him if he could build him a deck. When that second deck was finished, it too was not looking bad. It was solid, safe, and serving its purpose. It was not perfect, but it was *good enough*. It was not long until a third request came in for a deck. Not wanting to disappoint, it was constructed in a timely fashion. When that third deck was finished, it was looking good. It was solid, safe, and serving its purpose. It was not perfect, but it was *good enough*. For the builder, the third deck was the best one. He had built it using his time efficiently because he had developed a system. He used the tools to their maximum capacity, creating minimal effort. The mistakes that he made building the first two decks were not repeated. In all three cases, it would take an expert eye to spot mistakes in any of the three decks, and only the builder would have an increased sense of security when standing on the third deck. For everyone else, the decks were constructed *good enough*.

What I'm saying is all three decks were good enough, but one of them was closer to perfection than the others. Good enough comes from the value of the process along the way and the discovery of doing something that has value and provides results. As you get better, previous standards of good enough become fairly easy. The notion of perfection is always within grasp but never attained because you can always get better. In math, you are constantly limited because you have to restart until it's perfect.

Nat: How can we say something is *closer* to perfection if that perfection doesn't exist? This was the major sticking point in our conversations. Stéphan set up perfection as an asymptote to be approached but never reached. He not only had his own definition of perfection, he also had a completely different notion of mathematics. To him, mathematics was bound by a prescription of rules. Each step must be carefully executed or the perfection would be jeopardized. Ironically, this is how I view the process of welding. What it boiled down to was a state of being. In Stéphan's terms, the pathway through a problem or task is filled with a constant recalibration and self-evaluation. To him, these recalibrations always stood in between him and perfection. This process, I would assume, is what he considers learning. For me, perfection is a personal movement or synchronization between someone and their task. While there may be no archetype for a *perfect deck*, the essence of perfection evolves alongside the learner. The person forms their idea of a perfect deck as they go along. In turn, the pathway toward perfection also shapes the person. It is a mutual process. This notion of constant, prescriptive perfection is what creates the aura of rationalism around mathematics and begins to separate the core subjects from the options. I do not think mathematics and welding are worlds apart. In both, it requires a high degree of creativity within proscriptive boundaries to truly master the craft, and, in both, I see perfection emerging as the act and the actor co-implicate.

What Roles Do Creativity and Rigor Play in Your Subject Area?

Nat: Stéphan spoke very passionately about creativity during our many conversations, and often as the opposite of rigor. For me, rigor is an adherence to careful exactness while creativity is a sort of license with the tools of the craft. Math classes (in high school) are too focused on the idea of exactness, and efforts to imbue creativity result in tokenism toward the options classes. It is as though mathematics can borrow some application from a practical discipline like woodworking or welding, and, in return, grant it some respect from a more rigorous perch. I once had my students do a home remodeling project where they were required to decide on certain upgrades to flooring, furniture, and architecture and then prepare a budget for the renovation. Part of the project required detailed calculations for the surface area of the walls to be painted. Not long thereafter, my wife and I decided to paint our master bedroom. When it came time to buy paint, we based our purchase on rough overestimations. School mathematics clings to rigor and uses situated contexts as creative boosters. In this sense, creativity and rigor do stand opposed to one another. I would prefer to speak of the self-contained creativity in mathematics; it is this nature of mathematics that allows us to play (create) within the exactness (rigor) of the mathematical.

Stéphan: Even though it is important to have a certain balance in the classroom. The fact is that I learn just as much from the students as they learn from me. I am always amazed to see how passionate students get when they fall in love with something. How many times have I learned new skills because I was not able to say no to students? Students ask to build skateboards, but I don't know the first thing about it. By the end of the project, we have a skateboard, a relationship, new skills for the students and myself, and a mutual respect. I would even go further and say that the learning was cooperative, and it comes with great advantages.

> It is effective in promoting higher academic achievements with a deeper understanding of learned material, better high-level reasoning and critical thinking skills, better development of interpersonal and social skills, increasing abilities to view situations from others' perspectives, more supportive relationships with peers, lower levels of anxiety and stress, and greater intrinsic motivation to learn. (Navarro-Pabloa & Gallardo-Saboridob, 2015)

True freedom is required to allow them to find different ways to get to different destinations. In math, I would assume that freedom is granted in order to find different ways to get a rigid predetermined answer to a problem or a situation. In reality, there is not much freedom, and so not much room for real creativity. It is only an illusion; at the end of the day students need to converge to a specific answer. For this reason, I think that real creativity needs to be conjoined with freedom.

Nat: I like Stéphan's use of the word *freedom* in tandem with *creativity*, but would disagree with the necessity of what he calls *true freedom*. I do so on two grounds. First, if we are to employ our crafts vocationally (in school or in life) we always have a job to do. Whether this is building a deck or solving for an unknown, there is a point when we can say the job has been completed to a certain standard (regardless you believe in perfect standards or not). There is never a true freedom in our actions in school; budgets, assessments, and time all legislate restrictions but do not completely eliminate freedom. Second, even if one were to engage in an activity purely for aesthetic pleasure, you are bound by the tools of the craft.

Both welding and mathematics have tools that can be employed for standard purposes, and used creatively when used in non-routine situations. Even when engaging in fanciful play, freedom is limited by the tools. In this way, the tools contain the rigor and the utilization of the tools can be termed creativity. The freedom to act within the boundaries of these tools is what I think of as creativity. Think of a hammer; it has certain structural limitations and is designed for a specific purpose. This represents the rigor of the tool. A hammer can be used as many things when completing a job. It can be a lever, a counter-weight, an anvil, or—as my dad has demonstrated numerous times—it can even be a screwdriver. Here we see the creativity, and perhaps impatience, of the actor. True, unbridled freedom is always bound by the tools of the trade. In this way, I think of rigor and freedom as nested phenomena (Fig. 3.1). The tools retain their rigor, but enable creativity when in action. Here, creativity doesn't stand opposed to rigor, but is nested around it.

Stéphan: When I think of creativity, I think of a situation where you can process without constraint and restriction. It is here where you can imagine and innovate without pressures of working toward an absolute in an environment where you will not be afraid to take risks. The result is truly about the process, and the process gets better as you improve the results. The most efficient process is gained through experience. Many times I have had a student ask me if they can make their own project. I reluctantly agree, but assume they will only come up with a decent result.

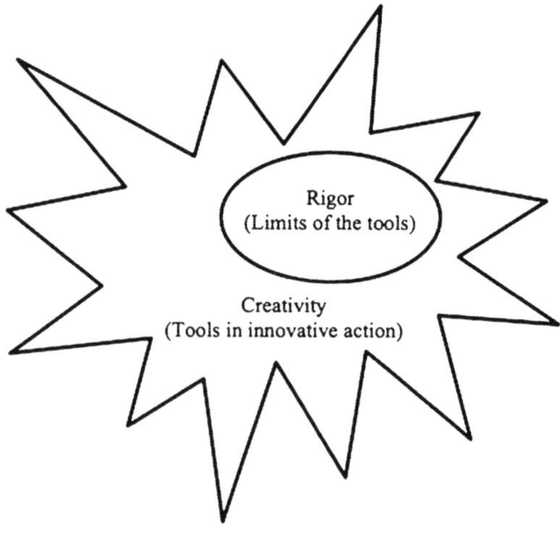

Fig. 3.1 Nat's model of creativity and rigor. Creativity emerges from innovative use of rigorous tools

Every year I get caught in this trap, and every year students surprise me with fantastic results. Creativity allows the worker to correct old mistakes while, at the same time, searching for new methods. In the options, creativity reinvents efficiency.

Nat: George Dantzig was a student at UC Berkeley running late for a course in advanced statistics. When he arrived, there were two problems written on the blackboard. He copied them down and spent days working toward solutions he found to be more difficult than usual. Weeks after submission, Dantzig's professor knocked on his door. He had prepared an introduction to his proof to be sent off for publication. Unknowingly, Dantzig had completed the two problems that the professor had used as examples of unsolved problems in statistics (Albers & Reid, 1986). Maybe this is the perfect example of taking creative risks, but it took the ignorance of the context to allow Dantzig to operate freely. He didn't deviate from the statistical tools (rigor) but utilized them in unorthodox ways (creativity). The result was a degree of freedom that allowed him to complete something that had stumped the most brilliant statisticians of the day. Again, creativity emerged from rigor (see Fig. 3.1). The difference here is creativity was used to converge on a solution—a right answer. After the dust settles, the proofs that were unsuccessful are markedly different than the builder's first two decks in your story. Your story ends with three unique decks, mine ends with three unique proofs only one of which served its ultimate purpose.

Stéphan: I see rigor constantly occurring when we are creating, solving, and working through problems. In a way, I see it as opposite. Rigor emerges from creativity (Fig. 3.2). I am implying that we need to be rigorous in everything we do in life or it quickly loses its purpose. The tools Nat speaks of need to be born somewhere; they emerge from creativity. New problems require new solutions. How many times has sideways thinking created a new solution to a problem? Nat just demonstrated it with Dantzig's example, but it exists in commonplace examples like sticky notes and spray insulation. They are now (rigorous) industry standards, but they began as innovations. While it may seem that rigor is built through convergent, perfect steps, it is actually established through divergent thoughts that provide strategic advantage.

If we are to balance rigor in an environment built from creativity, we need to move rigor out from the implicit curriculum and into the explicit curriculum (Eisner, 1985). For too long, rigor has been considered an activity of the mind, born from rationalism. Having conversations with the

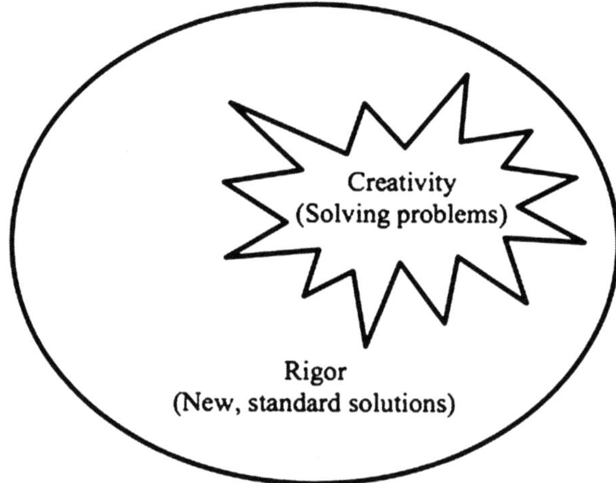

Fig. 3.2 Stéphan's model of creativity and rigor. Rigor is in every action and emerges from the work on problems

students about the nature of rigor and the habits of someone who values rigor would position them in a reflective position. They get the tools to think flexibly in a metacognitive way while continuing to question and solve problems. Every action as a learner involves rigor and making this fact explicit would move the notion of rigor outside of specific subjects and into the realm of lifelong learning.

How Do You Frame the Notion of Intelligence?

Nat: Fifth grade was an important one for me and my developing worldview of intelligence. The teacher told me that I could work ahead into the grade six math textbook because I was so far ahead. I really only knew one thing about math at that point—I was really good at it. I was allowed to work ahead because I was intelligent. I believed intelligence was locally housed; it was an individual attribute constructed through interactions but abstracted until it can be utilized by an individual, regardless of situation. The history of past problems cannot be forgotten, but the milieu in which they existed must be. This rational disembodiment is what creates the aura of objectivism in math. The student who can ignore distraction (both inward and outward) is the one that can intelligently connect the necessary links to solve problems, and solving problems was at the very heart of my juvenile understanding of intelligence.

Stéphan: There is such a variance in defining intelligence I would rather use the word *harmony*. I think of intelligence as a process we can use to act within a system productively. Intelligence is then the ability to mesh with the system and contribute to its advancement. Technology is a prime example. Think of how tablets have slowly made their way into the everyday functions of this world. This relatively new technology allows us to operate smoother—more intelligently. On a more humanistic note, we attempt to achieve harmony every time we play a team sport. We meet with new teammates, learn their strengths and their weaknesses, and mesh together in order to contribute to the competitive advancement of the team. I think of it being an adaptation process, picking the right tool out of the toolbox for a task whether it is simple or complex. It is not a matter of being a smooth operator and solving many problems. Rather, an intelligent or harmonious person understands the many consequences of their actions and uses the many tools to create profitable change and solve necessary problems. I played a decent level of hockey growing up. I would make a point of coming to the rink early to watch the game or practice before ours. I always found that it was a good way to get ready for my own practices or games. It would help me focus by watching how other players would act in certain situations; it helped me learn because I was seeing the game through other players. I could see the whole ice, and pinpoint ways in which player action helped the team. I was no longer focused on flashy individual plays; the change of scope allowed me to focus on the intelligence of a larger system—a team.

Nat: I think we agree on this topic more than the others. Perhaps this is a harmony all in itself? It is said great (or intelligent) minds think alike. Unfortunately, that means unintelligent minds might also share brainwaves. I'm hoping we are the former.

Before my grandfather died, I remember sitting around a campfire at the family farm and asking him questions about his life. My family and I had moved across the country and I had been largely alienated from the farming lifestyle. I asked him, if he could go back and do it all over again, would he change anything? He paused for a second and with his patented sigh, replied, "Oh, no. I don't think so". I then asked him why he chose farming. It was hard work with unpredictable results. My grandfather was a brilliant man with a quick wit and a huge heart for others. Why wouldn't he chose to pursue something more than continuing a family farm? He replied, “Why be smart if it doesn’t help anyone?” Farming gave him the opportunity to put his mind into action, and the result was a notion of active intelligence. An intelligent person has the ability to solve problems in novel ways. It does not take intelligence to apply a set procedure repeatedly in a familiar context. Unfortunately, math class often boils down to this. I was branded as *intelligent* because of my high rates of accuracy and automaticity. Correct answers were important, but only impressive if they were done with a high rate of speed. By way of illustration, I was recently talking with a young girl who had just finished grade one. I asked her if she liked math class, and she replied that her friend Josh must like it because he is always done first.

Stéphan: Intelligence does not have an individual identity; an individual might apply it, but I think it comes from a collective mind. No ideas or inventions are truly original; they are always created through an outside source. That source could be in the form of another’s opinion or viewpoint or come from something that was there before, whether it is a problem or a situation. We see it when an invention is used to fix a problem it never intended to, or an idea is taken from a field (say, psychology), and adapted to fit another (say, education). We cannot escape the shoulders of giants.

That is the core of this duoethnography. It takes us (as a collective) to really operate intelligently on our views. If this was a memoir, it would quickly become a sermon about our personal histories as they exist in isolation. For this reason, I found my answers in this section to hold little personal relevance. I don’t think the notion of intelligence should be framed by any particular subject (Gardner, 1993), but should be a holistic measure of how individuals act on a system to move it forward while retaining harmony within it. My answer to the question “How do you frame the notion of intelligence?” is *I don’t bother*.

Nat: The ideas of harmony and collective intelligence resonate with me, but I know that the school system would not agree. I find myself on opposing sides of a war that cannot be won. On one side, we have the structure of schools with individual grades, standardized assessments, and valedictory addresses. On the other, we have the idea of intelligence as collective, harmonious action. School was rarely harmonious for me, even in group projects. Group work was always accompanied with a subconscious tally of merit. I was always aware of who was doing the most difficult work. Although roles were not made explicit, leaders quickly emerged, and I was always aware of it. Duoethnography has revived many petty memories of my school days. For instance, I did my grade six science fair project with two of my best friends. We won the school contest and were entered into a district competition. Only two of us could go to the competition, and my teacher randomly chose; I was left out. I acted like I was fine with it, but I was very disappointed. My friends must have known because when we got selected for the provincial competition, they didn't tell me. We got in an argument on the school yard when I finally found out we won. They said they didn't tell me because they thought I would be mad. They were probably right. Not mad, but jealous. I was the brains of the operation. I deserved to go. It really doesn't matter now, but does show how situations that look harmonious are often undergirded with individualism.

After hearing Stéphan's notion of harmony, I wonder how harmonious my classroom looks? I know I value collectivity, but the final say is dictated by the bureaucratic tendencies of the school system. The legacy of school mathematics leaves its heaviest and most ugly stain on the concept of intelligence.

How Has the Duoethnographic Process Shifted Your Lens?

Stéphan: The application of duoethnography moves beyond the conversation; it is an introspection that made me recognize the true multiplicity in my classroom. It reiterates the fact that the classroom is not a stagnant monoculture; it is alive and kicking in every direction. I am lucky to be able to share a passion and witness the way the students are applying the skills that they learn. I do know that there is a space for every learning style in my classroom, but the reality is that we usually use our strengths in the way we teach. It is my job to make sure that I get the best out of every student whether they have an aptitude suited for science, language, mathematics, or the options. I need to initiate purposeful dialogue with students about their motivations, roadblocks, and self-identities. I think a lot of the practical fallout from the project comes in the form of dialogue, much like the process itself.

I wasn't able to truly acknowledge what I valued until the thoughts inside my head were challenged. I realized that I value a communal sense of intelligence and that means that a simple continuum from thinking to doing does not represent the atmosphere I want in my classroom. I will make efforts to connect students who are working on a similar project and asking similar questions. We will try to instigate a supportive system where I do not represent the correct idea, but we all contribute. Ideally, I want to create a process of thinking, reflecting, asking, and (ultimately) doing. This networking builds on the idea of communal or shared intelligence.

Nat: Conversational tension with Stéphan provided many stresses to my lens. Some of these are new things I hope to establish, and others are dormant beliefs that have been reawakened and need to be re-placed in a position of importance. They do not all exist as objects that can be placed neatly in lesson preparations and classroom structures, but exist as a heightened state of awareness having interrogated these key ideas. Admittedly, the first draft of my *applications* focused on specific problems and routines that fit with my expanded lens of right—notions of intelligence, harmony, and perfection. Upon further inspection, this record did not do the process justice. I feel this revision exemplifies the shift in my lens of *right*. Those applications diluted the learnings into linear and programmable steps no different than my fifth grade mad minutes.

Talking with Stéphan made me realize why it is I love mathematics and the perfection it holds. It is the connective intricacies that make mathematics vibrant for me. This reinforces my teaching. I also know that my view of intelligence has shifted more toward the idea of *harmony*. If mathematics is to truly grow and co-implicate with its user, intelligence needs to take on a quality of action. I want my students to work *with* mathematics instead of operating *on* mathematics. In this way, their intelligence is not static and measurable, but a state of being mathematical. Intelligence moves from a noun (built and stored over time) to a verb (shifting, enacting in context).

Looking for applications brings me back to the fictitious (but incredibly potent) conversation between a scientist and a novelist told by Ted Aoki (1993). Some would be tempted to try and reconcile the differences between the two, but I prefer to live in the tension between the core and optional subjects. This way, it reminds me what I value about the other.

Epilogue

The process of duoethnography was a *perfect* method to examine our deep-seated beliefs of education through our respective lenses. It forced an introspective analysis as conversations challenged our foundational beliefs. We served as mutual catalysts for thought, and emerged knowing one another deeply. We began by brainstorming possible ways to structure our differences so they could be effectively highlighted through our discussions, but they constantly shifted as we found our way to the heart of the issue for us. Duoethnography pulled at the issues honestly; there was no need (or even the possibility) to fabricate dichotomies of difference. They emerged fluidly.

This fluidity was frustrating for both parties. We found it exhausting to constantly chase ourselves as we built our new perspectives of *right*. The many meetings were not simple exchanges of views but rather a conversation where the ideas of the speaker and listener formed each other. The exchanges never turned antagonistic, but we were often able to help each other articulate beliefs because of our distant stance. At the heart of the process was the fact that we are both teachers, despite our differences.

The value of this process is impossible to measure. We do not say this as some kind of poetic concluding remark, but from the understanding that the conversations will continue to trigger a reflective engagement for both of us and hopefully others. Printing a copy to be assessed toward a credit in a program of studies seems artificial. It gives a strong impression of finality; this impression is not shared by either of us. This manuscript is far from *perfect*, but we hope it stands as *good enough*. Our last comment on the methodology is that duoethnography is a misnomer if executed correctly. The moment you start reading, you, as reader, become part of the conversation. It is our hope that this transcended the space of *duo* and moved into a *multi-ethnography*.

References

Albers, D. J., & Reid, C. (1986). An interview with George B. Dantzig: The father of linear programming. *College Mathematics Journal, 17*(4), 293–314.

Alberta Education. (2008). *Mathematics: Grades 10–12*. Retrieved from https://education.alberta.ca/media/655889/math10to12.pdf

Aoki, T. T. (1993). Legitimating live curriculum: Toward a curricular landscape of multiplicity. In W. Pinar & R. L. Irwin (Eds.), *Curriculum in a new key: The collected works of Ted T. Aoki*. New York, NY: Routledge.

Eisner, E. W. (1985). *The educational imagination: On the design and evaluation of school programs* (2nd ed.). New York, NY: Macmillan Publishing.

Flinders, D. J., Noddings, N., & Thornton, S. J. (1986). The null curriculum: Its theoretical basis and practical implications. *Curriculum Inquiry, 16*(1), 33–42.

Gardner, H. (1993). *Frames of mind: The theory of multiple intelligences* (Tenth anniversary ed.). New York, NY: BasicBooks.

Kieren, T., & Simmt, E. (2009). Brought forth in bringing forth. The inter-actions and products of a collective learning system. *Complicity: An International Journal of Complexity and Education, 6*(2), 20–28.

Krammer, D., & Mangiardi, R. (2012). The hidden curriculum of schooling: A duoethnographic exploration of what schools teach us about schooling. In J. Norris & R. D. Sawyer (Eds.), *Duoethnography: Dialogic methods for social, health, and educational research* (pp. 41–70). Walnut Creek, CA: Left Coast Press.

McLeod, J. (1987). The arts and education. In J. Simpson (Ed.), *Education and the arts*. Edmonton, AB: Fine Arts Council, Alberta Teachers' Association.

Mezirow, J. (2000). *Learning as transformation: Critical perspectives on a theory in progress*. San Francisco, CA: Jossey-Bass.

Navarro-Pablo, M., & Gallardo-Saborido, E. J. (2015). Teaching to training teachers through cooperative learning. *Procedia—Social And Behavioral Sciences, 180*, 401–406.

Norris, J. (2008). A quest for a theory and practice of authentic assessment: An arts based approach. *LEARNing Landscapes, 2*(1), 211–233.

Norris, J., & Sawyer, R. D. (2004). Null and hidden curricula of sexual orientation: A dialogue on the curreres of the absent presence and the present absence. In L. Coia, M. Birch, N. J. Brooks, E. Heilman, S. Mayer, A. Mountain, & P. Pritchard (Eds.), *Democratic responses in an era of standardization* (pp. 139–159). Troy, NY: Curriculum and Pedagogy.

Norris, J., & Sawyer, R. D. (2012). Toward a dialogic methodology. In J. Norris & R. D. Sawyer (Eds.), *Duoethnography: Dialogic methods for social, health, and educational research* (pp. 41–70). Walnut Creek, CA: Left Coast Press.

Proulx, J., & Simmt, E. (2013). Enactivism in mathematics education: Moving toward a re-conceptualization of learning and knowledge. *Education Sciences & Society, 4*(1), 59–79.

Robinson, K. (2001). *Out of our minds: Learning to be creative*. Chichester, England: Capstone Publishing Limited.

Scudder Jr., J. R. (1968). Freedom with authority: A Buber model for teaching. *Educational Digest, 34*(2), 28–31.

Smith, M. S., & Stein, M. (2011). *5 practice for orchestrating productive mathematics discussions*. Reston, VA: The National Council of Teachers of Mathematics.

Zack, V., & Reid, D. A. (2003). Good-enough understanding: Theorising about the learning of complex ideas (part 1). *For the Learning of Mathematics, 23*(3), 43–50.

CHAPTER 4

Dialogic Life History in Preservice Teacher Education

Rick Breault

There is little doubt that the occupation one chooses, the meaning given to that choice, and decisions made within that occupation are all influenced by one's life history. This is true across professions (Hilson, 2008; Sjølie, Karlsson, & Binder, 2013), cultures (Mpungose, 2010), and disciplines (McCulloch, Marshall, DeCuir-Gunby, & Caldwell, 2013). Perhaps nowhere, though, is the influence of life history more apparent and direct than in those who would be teachers. The self one brings to any occupation has been shaped by experiences in your life before that time. However, in fields like law, architecture, medicine, or aviation, practitioners have not been immersed in their future jobs in the way teachers have. As Knowles and Holt-Reynolds (1991) point out, "The influence of twelve years or more of observing and participating—often successfully—in 'status quo' school and university classrooms introduces a tension unique to teacher education" (p. 88).

In his sociological study of teaching, Lortie (1975) suggested that it "strains imagination to picture a child making a well-reasoned career choice at the age of eight or ten-years-old" (p. 42). Yet, many future teachers do indeed make their career choice at that time. Unlike nearly

R. Breault (✉)
Ashland University, Ashland, OH, USA

J. Norris, *Theorizing Curriculum Studies, Teacher Education, and Research through Duoethnographic Pedagogy*,
DOI 10.1057/978-1-137-51745-6_4

every other occupational choice "teaching possesses recruitment resources beyond its relative attractiveness in cost and benefit terms" (Lortie, 1975, p. 42). It is the power of the identification with and relationships to teachers and family members who are teachers that lead young people to picture themselves as teachers from a very early age. The impact of life history on one's chosen profession goes far beyond the initial decision to become a teacher, or nurse, or psychotherapist. As Sjølie et al. (2013) discovered in their study of specialized nursing teams in Norway, "They [their life experiences] give meaning to the relationship between themselves as people and the work role, work experiences, and their family experiences when relating these experiences to their current work" (p. 12). The same sort of relationships have been found in studying autobiographical influences on preservice teachers.

A Lifelong Methods Course

A significant body of research has shown that the notion of self a preservice teacher brings to formal teacher preparation is a powerful determinant of later pedagogical beliefs and practices. What makes this phenomenon so challenging to teacher educators is that the preservice teacher's life history does not just develop certain personality traits; it shapes even how one teaches, manages the classroom, and/or chooses to implement or ignore new reforms (Clark, 1988; Cole, 1990; Ebbs, 1997; Knowles, 1992).

Britzman (1991) described the process of learning how to teach as "a time when one's past, present and future are set in dynamic tension" (p. 8). The present learning of any future teacher is filtered first through their past experiences. Those past experiences or "apprenticeship of observation" (Lortie, 1975) include thousands of hours spent observing teacher behaviors in a wide variety of settings. The pedagogical actions of teachers observed during that time are all the more powerful because those teachers are often highly respected, even loved, by the young future teacher. For some young people the teachers from whom they learned what it means to be a teacher might also have been a parental substitute, a first crush, an admired coach or even a loving parent. As a result, what was a simple apprenticeship can be inextricably embedded in an emotionally satisfying time spent with a beloved and caring adult.

The role of life history would not be problematic if it meant simply that future teachers came to professional education with a predisposition to want to be a good teacher. Instead, ample research shows that what was learned during those years of apprenticeship of observation eventually become "lay theories" (Holt-Reynolds, 1992) which are then translated into specific teaching practices that are not easily changed (Beauchamp & Thomas, 2009; Calderhead & Robson, 1991; Furlong, 2013; Hammerness, Darling-Hammond, & Bransford, 2005; Vacc & Bright, 1999). Preservice teachers do not consciously learn those lay theories "at an announced, recognized moment from a formal teaching/learning episode" (Holt-McReynolds, 1992, p. 326). They are powerful enough, however, that when they clash with more progressive notions presented in formal teacher education the tension produced is likely to be a barrier to innovation and policy change (Eick & Reed, 2001).

Nurturing Critical Awareness

More often than not because lay theories and dispositions develop in a gradual and largely unrecognized way they go unexamined or even noticed by the future teacher (Azevedo & Cromley, 2004; Bullough & Gitlin, 2001; Stooksberry, Schussler, & Bercaw, 2009). The new teacher's pedagogical decisions can end up being "merely appetitive, blind and impulsive" (Dewey, 1933, p. 17). The challenge for teacher educators is to help preservice teachers become critically aware of their existing beliefs and assumptions so that they can better determine the impact on decision-making and teacher identity. Awareness alone, however, is not sufficient.

> Teaching has to do, in part at least, with the formation of beliefs, and that means that it has to do not simply with what we shall believe, but with how we shall believe it. Teaching is an activity which has to do, among other things, with the modification and formation of beliefs systems. (Green, 1971, p. 48)

Bringing about deepening awareness and understanding is no easy task. Numerous studies show that, if changes in beliefs occur at all, the process is challenging (Kagen, 1992; Pajares, 1992; Peacock, 2001; Polat, 2010; Raths, 2001; Stofflett & Stoddart, 1994; Weinstein, 1989). While there is no consensus on the potential of teacher education to bring about changes in perceptions and assumptions, those efforts that appear to have been successful in doing so have yielded some activities and environmental characteristics needed to increase the likelihood of change.

Using duoethnography with preservice teachers is based on the premise that teaching dispositions and philosophy are developmental, evolutionary projects that are constructed and reconstructed over time (Edmunson, 1990; Jacobs & Duhon-Sells, 1994; Levison, 1974; Stookesbury et al., 2009; Wisdom, 1963). It is even possible that too much attention to assessing dispositions early in teacher preparation programs will redirect attention away from increasing candidates' awareness and development of dispositions over time. Instead, preservice programs need to "operate programmatically, building sequentially and individually on candidates' awareness of their dispositions" (Stookesbury et al., 2009, p. 732).

While there are any number of dispositions we would like to have teacher candidates to possess, my purpose in using duoethnography in teacher education is "less about changing one's moral filter than about helping candidates develop awareness that they possess this filter" (Stookesbury et al., 2009, p. 728). Moreover, it is also crucial to discover why and how they have constructed the beliefs that have (Polat, 2010). Duoethnography is particularly well-suited to address this need.

The Context

Two groups of students were involved in the pilot project described in this chapter. A serendipitous schedule meant that I had two groups of preservice teachers in two different classes that differed in significant ways. It is important to note that this was not initially intended as a study to compare the results of both groups. The intention of the project was the same in both groups—to promote autobiographical insight into one's future teaching decisions. The manner in which I approached duoethnography varied according to the limitations and nature of each course. Still, I believe important insights came from comparing the respective approaches and the differences suggest some more and less effective uses of duoethnography to promote reflection.

One group came from an undergraduate teacher education track and was enrolled in a course taken just prior to formal admission to the teacher education program. The enrollment included students who were interested in both elementary and secondary education and covered the topics typical of "Introduction to Education" courses everywhere—the nature of curriculum and instruction, key concepts and issues in public education, what it means to be a teacher, and so on. Students in the course were also expected to participate in volunteer activities involving children and the community at sites such as daycare centers, 4-H, Park District programs, and tutoring centers. While there were common goals and activities across sections of the course which was taught to a number of graduate students and faculty, instructors were free to put their own slant on the course and could assign additional work or some different readings. In my section of the class I opted for an emphasis on the perceptions one brings to the beginning of teacher preparation programs and on nurturing the metacognitive process to develop greater insight into how and what you are learning during the preservice teacher education process.

The undergraduate class consisted of 19 students, 3 male and 16 female, one of whom was African-American. About half the group were secondary education majors from a variety of disciplines. All were traditionally aged undergraduate students and all but three were native to the state. Several were from the same school districts. The results reported in this project are based on the responses of only 14 students. The remaining five either did not complete the course or did not consent to be a part of the research.

Due to the wide range of topics required in the course and the limited time available I was not able to devote much in-class time to the duoethnography. This turned out to be an important factor in the final quality of the effort. The majority of conversation time took place outside of class at the convenience of the students. There was very little in-class discussion of the abbreviated duoethnographies. Another reflective, writing-intensive assignment—an educational belief statement—required a lot of the class time that was available beyond the content of the class since it tended to be more difficult for the students. During this same semester the students were required to develop an application portfolio. While the content was largely independent of the class, by default, this was the class in which questions about the portfolio were addressed. In hindsight, those factors detracted from what could have been done with the duoethnography.

The second group were also preservice teachers but in this case the class consisted of eight graduate students pursuing certification through an alternative Masters of Arts in teaching program. The students were recent college graduates in their mid to late twenties. Their undergraduate degrees were in English, foreign languages, history, and math. The class, *Educational Philosophy,* had a more narrow focus than the undergraduate course. Moreover, the focus I chose for the class was on thinking "philosophically" about your own teaching rather than on the content of various educational philosophies. Most of the students in this class had experience as graduate teaching assistants, coaches, or teaching assistants in local schools. These differences were obviously factors in interpreting the results of the project.

Jump-starting the Process

The duoethnography for the undergraduates consisted of four parts: preparation, conversation, writing, and follow-up. The preparation or groundwork for the conversation was intended to take place before the beginning of the semester while most students would be spending at least some time at home or with family over the winter break between semesters. A few weeks before the semester in which the duoethnography was assigned the students were sent a letter via e-mail that provided a brief explanation of the autobiographical activities they would be doing in the class and suggested some preparation they could do jump-start the process.

> Since the activity relies primarily on memory, and we know that memories tend to get lost or "adapted" to fit what we want to remember, it is helpful to have some artifacts that will spur your recollections ... you might want to search for items related to past school experiences or other related experiences that contributed to your future teaching identify

- School artifacts: Yearbooks, report cards, old assignments, letters of recognition or honors, books, notes to or from friends or teachers, diaries, programs from special events, and so on.
- Photos related to school events and friends, or that tell you something about how you were shaped into a teacher (pictures of you reading, playing school, playing games or dolls, playing sports, vacations, etc.).
- Family recollections or stories.
- Items that might speak to personality traits that will be part of your teaching identity (artwork, stories you wrote, how you arranged your room, evidence of involvement in volunteer activities, etc.).

The reason for artifacts is twofold. First, they can help students recall specific incidents, put a visual context to a memory, or retrace developmental processes as they look at childhood images of themselves (Norris & Sawyer, 2012). Another purpose of the artifacts is to serve as a check on the authenticity and reliability of memory.

Given the already noted unfamiliarity with reflective exercises in the same pre-semester letter I asked the students to recall well-remembered events from their own educational experiences.

> Try to recall one true story ... that captures the "essence" of your experience as a student in elementary, middle, and/or high school. This can be a story about an interaction with other students, a conversation with a teacher, an emotionally-charged event, or other such things. ... It can be funny, happy, thought-provoking, or just representative of who you are and indicative of how you might react to students.

A "well-remembered event", as described by Carter (1993), is "an incident or episode a student observes in a school situation and considers, for his or her own reasons, especially salient or memorable" (p. 7). According to Carter, it is common for those preservice teachers to hold those stories close and make them into a theory on which they base later teaching decisions. Therefore, it was hoped that if they could recall one or more of these events and bring them to the initial duoethnographic conversations, the process would have a meaningful starting point.

No preparatory letter was sent to the graduate class. Since the process used with the graduate students was more prolonged, I suggested seeking out artifacts and stories that could be used as the conversation continued. This was not a pedagogical decision as much as it was a logistical one based on when I was asked to do the class and the time available before it would begin. The difference proved to be inconsequential, however, since few of the undergraduate students read the early e-mail or sought out any artifacts.

Structuring the Conversations

> The syllabi for both courses contained only a brief description of duoethnography: "This is a two-person process in which, through a probing, reflective conversation, you will create an educational autobiography. The focus will be on linking your past experiences to your current perceptions and beliefs about school, learning, students, and teaching".

The way in which the conversations would proceed was described to the undergraduate group during class. In this case they chose their own conversation partner or could ask to be paired with another student who did not have a partner. The same was true for the graduate group. Conducting a true duoethnography with a complete stranger is not recommended because of the trust and comfort needed to explore the issues that might arise. In some cases there were students in class who knew each other and there was a noticeable difference in the content and depth of the conversation in those cases. In the classroom setting I was not as concerned with the quality of the conversation partners since the purpose was simply to spark a more intentionally reflective process through conversation through a relatively short and focused process. I did not anticipate the depth of exploration that would occur in a more research-oriented, purposeful, and voluntary duoethnography.

The undergraduate duoethnography was limited to a one-time, one-hour conversation guided by nine specific prompts. They did not have to address each prompt. They were intended only as suggested conversation starters.

1. Share your most memorable experiences from your time in school and why you think those experiences were so memorable.
2. Why did you choose to become a teacher?
3. To what extent did your own decision to teach grow out of your experiences as a student?
4. What were your strengths and weaknesses as a student?
5. How did you learn most effectively? Least effectively?
6. What did you enjoy most and least about going to school?
7. Which teachers were your favorites? Why?
8. What messages did your family communicate about the importance of school? What about your community?
9. What outside (non-school) experiences or influences might have shaped the kind of student you were and the kind of teacher you will be?

With the graduate class I used a more directed and extended process that I referred to as a "progressive duoethnography". Only four prompts were suggested and they were assigned over a period of several weeks. The conversation pair was to address one question at a time, although they could return to previous question if they wish to add to or revisit previous responses. The prompts, in order, were:

1. Begin with autobiographical background and list some questions about the other person's background that you would like to pursue further.
2. Do you consider yourself a "philosophical" person?

3. What are some of your key beliefs about how people learn and can you identify some of the autobiographical experiences that might have influenced those beliefs.
4. What are the internal and external factors that might promote or hinder your becoming more "philosophical" about your teaching? (Internal: personal/intellectual qualities—External: background factors, workplace conditions, expectations of others, etc.)

Some of the prompts obviously lent themselves to a variety of definitions and directions and the students were encouraged to define those directions for themselves. For example, they could pursue what it means to be "philosophical" in their own ways. In each case, though, the participants were encouraged to illustrate or explore their responses in terms of autobiographical events and influences.

Considering the Conversations

In duoethnography the insights and transformations occur primarily within the conversations (Norris & Sawyer, 2012). In both classes, the conversational phase of the process concluded with a summary of and reflection on the results and value of the process. I added this step as one last chance to consider what happened during the conversations and the extent to which the pair was really listening and considering what was said and to which each person was integrating new perspectives into his or her own stories as the conversation progressed. As part of that process the students were asked to search their stories for the impact they might have on their preparation as teachers and on their future effectiveness in the classroom. Here, too, I offered prompts to guide their reflections. Some suggestions included:

- Can you identify existing beliefs or ideas about teaching and schooling in general that are rooted in the stories you told about your early education experiences?
- What biases might you bring to the classroom that could be either beneficial or detrimental to your effectiveness as a teacher? Remember, the word "bias" can imply prejudice or partiality, but it can also refer to your preferences, particular ways of viewing the world, and so on, in a neutral or even positive way. How might you need to compensate for or adapt yourself to the biases you hold?

- How might your own experiences be used to help you understand or meet the needs of your future students?
- Do you see your educational experiences as being similar to or different from the students you are most likely to teach?
- Are there questions you have about your own education or past experiences you want to investigate as a result of this activity? If so, what are they?

Mixed Results and Lessons Learned

As originally conceived the project was intended to help students recollect past educational experiences and view them in relation to the experiences of other preservice teachers. At this level there is clear evidence that the project succeeded. Every student in both classes was able to recount memorable educational experiences and, with the exception of a few undergraduate students who submitted incomplete projects, all students were able to recount what they considered to be the most important recollections of their duoethnography partners. There were obvious differences, however, regarding the extent to which those shared stories were heard *in relation to* each other or in a way that one person's stories informed or shaped the recollection of the other person. The difference was most noticeable when comparing the results of the undergraduate group to the graduate preservice teachers.

When asked to write a summary of their duoethnographies at least half the summaries included what could be considered thorough and reflective accounts of their personal educational biographies. However, those read more like chronological or stream-of-consciousness recollections than the results of a dialogue and only four of the undergraduates described the process in a way that deliberately compared and contrasted the experiences of their partners. More common was simply retelling two parallel stories, as though they were just telling their stories in turn with little indication of a conversation. There also seemed to be little connection made to the influence of the personal experiences on their future teaching. In contrast, several students did describe a process that captured the spirit of the exercise in a way that I would have hoped.

> I have been to many places in the world; these places have given me a better understanding for teaching. Cathy, on the other hand, has never even been outside of the east coast. She has specific views on teaching because

> she has only ever witnessed one way. ... I am a very outgoing girl who loves kids and is extremely patient. Cathy ... is not patient and gets stressed out very easily, but she has an amazing way of showing kids how to get answers to math problems. This is a very big weakness of mine I have never been a good problem solver and being a teacher I know that is a big task I need to learn more on [Brenda]
>
> Julianne said, "I will tap into my past experiences as a teacher pretty often. I think I will remember the things I liked to do when I was in school and try to do more of those and at the same time stay away from the things that I know I did not learn anything from. Also I think I will try to use some of the same techniques as my favorite teachers". I think I'll probably tap into past experiences pretty frequently in teaching, but this isn't necessarily a bad thing. While it's of course important to have original and creative teaching styles in the classroom, it's also necessary and helpful to draw from what you know [Annie]

In those examples the students not only viewed the stories in relation to each other, they also referred to specific statements in their conversations and even offered some implications for their future teaching.

Greater evidence that the process of recollection was an interactive one with at least some sense of the "ethnography" in duoethnography was found in the assignment in which students were given directive prompts for thinking about the process. In reflecting on the process itself, comments like those below were the exception but still speak to the potential of the process as a meaningful tool for reflection.

> Answering the questions asked by my partner was challenging and thought-provoking. I was forced harder to examine how my background of education has guided me to wanting to be in Agriculture Education (Stacy)
>
> I have always had an idea about what kind of teacher I hoped to be, but what I now realize is how much of what I want to be as a teacher is based on who I was as a student. ... After reliving my educational journey through this assignment I have realized that as a student when I had a teacher I didn't respect, or felt that I was given assignments that were irrelevant I acted out or neglected to do my homework (Linda)
>
> I can remember when you were explaining the purpose and idea of the duoethnography on the first day of class. I have to admit that I could not see where this project would end up. I could not see what we were going to learn from it. It was not until I had actually completed my conversation that I realized how this assignment was beneficial. It allowed for me to see what I thought was the most influential experiences of my education and

> also what I believed were the least influential. ... Personally, I believe that if I remember my own education and the experiences I had, I will be able to better understand the needs and actions of my students (Stephanie)

Investigating the Differences

Several aspects of the duoethnography differed significantly from the graduate preservice teachers in terms of how they seemed to use the conversations and the post-conversation reflections. It would be easy to attribute the differences to developmental factors and life experiences of each group, but there were also differences in educational background and professional aspirations that cannot be ignored. All the graduate preservice participants had been prepared in a content area without an eye to k-12 teaching. Moreover, as explained earlier, the graduate group was taught in the context of an educational philosophy class and using a more deliberate and sequential approach to the duoethnography.

Since the basic topics being explored were different it would be difficult to argue that the graduate students' recollections or resulting implications for future teaching were somehow deeper or more insightful than those of the undergraduate students. However, as they summarized and reflected on their conversations there was more awareness of the dynamics of the relationship and how it might differ from other reflective exercises with similar goals. Consider, for instance, their greater awareness and importance of the conversational partner. While a number of students in the undergraduate group compared their experiences to someone else's and saw value in the process, the graduate students referred more directly to how the dialogic nature of duoethnography led to deeper insight.

> There were a few moments in our conversations where I would have to stop and think because I had never really considered something the way that she considers it. ... I was hesitant at the beginning of this project. I am happy to say at the end, however, that I really have learned a lot throughout this process. Although you mentioned that it might be somewhat weird due to the fact that we all didn't really know each other, I loved watching my friendship with Tamara grow and seeing how our conversations changed (Michelle)
>
> I discovered that while I thought I knew a lot about myself, my conversations forced me to be able to think outside of myself and see things from her point of view. I honestly believe that you cannot really understand or support your own views unless you have made an attempt to understand someone else's. ... I think that in addition to helping me understand the

> reasoning behind many of my beliefs, this process has reminded me of the beauty that comes with listening to and acknowledging someone else's as well (Kate)
>
> Having Amy as a part of this dialogue really helped me to learn more about myself through our shared experiences as well as our experiences which were dissimilar. Having another person to bounce ideas off of and compare to, especially someone like Amy who has teaching experience was definitely a rewarding experience (Alyssa)

Whereas the undergraduate students simply noted differences in each other's experiences as they told their respective stories, the graduate students used the process to, as one put it, "play each other's, devil's advocate". Past research on the reflective process suggests that the shared recollections of the undergraduates might have increased the participants' basic awareness of potential influences but probing, challenging use of dialogue by the graduate students resulted in deeper awareness or new insights into actual beliefs (Henderson, 2001; Levin, 2003; Raths & McAninch, 2003). The latter better reflects the goals I had for the project so it was important to examine the differences in each setting so as to use duoethnography more effectively in future attempts and better challenge preservice teachers to explore their latent assumptions and influences earlier in their development as teachers.

The most obvious difference would be the developmental and experiential differences in thinking between 19-year-old undergraduates and 25-plus-year-old graduate students (Perry, 1999). The tendency of beginning undergraduate students to view all activities as assignments to be checked off and to see the more "philosophical" or theoretical aspects of preservice education as irrelevant made it less likely that they would seriously engage in the duoethnography. However, those factors are not standard or immutable characteristics and it is important to consider the contextual and pedagogical factors that could have nurtured greater depth of thought and insight. So rather than take a more superficial "What worked and what didn't work" approach to the effectiveness of the duoethnography in each class I began with a loosely constructed conceptual framework from which to guide the post-course reflections and suggest revisions for the future. More specifically, borrowing from Lave and Wenger (1991) and, to a lesser extent, Bandura (1977), I wanted to look more closely at the kind of social engagements that might provide the proper context for the duoethnographer in a preservice education program.

Situating the Duoethnography

Teacher education programs have long asked preservice teachers to reflect on the influence of past experiences as learners. Often, however, those reflections take the form of individual "philosophy" statements or independent reflective essays. The use of tools such as duoethnography or collaborative autoethnography can increase the power of those reflections by juxtaposing self and collective analysis by conducting the reflections within "two seemingly contradictory frames of reference" and adding "rigor to autobiographical interrogation" (Chang, Ngunjiri, & Hernandez, 2013, p. 25). In order to promote that kind of autobiographical interrogation, though, the setting in which it takes place must be perceived as a safe, caring, and supportive environment (Carter & Doyle, 1996).

The environment in which the graduate students conducted their duoethnographies was much closer to that ideal than was that of the undergraduates so the more meaningful results should not be a surprise. The graduate group was smaller, they were further along in their program of study and had formed a de facto cohort with some of the fellow students, and the class met for three-hour sessions which made it more conducive to prolonged discussion and the forming of more trusting relationships between both peers and the teacher. The curriculum was also less structured and allowed for pursuing topics of interest. The undergraduate group met for about 90 minutes, included more students, and had a full slate of topics with numerous lengthy departmental requirements. Much more time was spent transmitting instructions and monitoring the format of those requirements. Moreover, few students knew each other from other classes. All these factors, including time of day and classroom setting, made the creation of trusting and close relationships much less likely. Little about their context promoted meaningful engagement or rigorous autobiographical interrogation even for those who would have liked to do so.

Duoethnography requires trust and nurtures mutual learning if the method is to be meaningful and if the process is meaningful the results can provide powerful insight into your pedagogical beliefs and practice and that of others. So as I reflected on how I might use duoethnography more effectively and consistently and where it might fit in context of the larger teacher education curriculum, what came to mind was notion-situated learning and communities of practice (CoPs) (Lave & Wenger, 1991; Lave & Chaiklin, 1993; Wenger, 1998, 1999). A strong pedagogical CoP would create the context necessary for fruitful duoethnography and fruitful duoethnography could make a significant contribution to the development of the community.

Duoethnography in Community

Since preservice classrooms do not typically consist of practitioners of various levels of experience sharing professional craft knowledge and learning from each other, they are not CoPs, as currently defined. However, it has been observed that CoP is an evolving concept that can be used to provide some guidance for the development of groups, teams, and networks (Li et al., 2009). Smith (2003) summarized the activity of CoP as members involved

> in a set of relationships over time and communities develop around things that matter to people. The fact that they are organizing around some particular area of knowledge and activity gives members a sense of joint enterprise and identity. For a community of practice to function it needs to generate and appropriate a shared repertoire of ideas, commitments and memories. It also needs to develop various resources such as tools, documents, routines, vocabulary and symbols that in some way carry the accumulated knowledge of the community. (p. 2)

In this setting the members of the community do not contribute to each other's pedagogical decision-making but they do work together to navigate the process of becoming teachers. They are organized around the knowledge and process of developing a pedagogical identity and the skills that accompany it. They are, or could be, generating a shared repertoire of ways to look at what it means to be a teacher and to thrive in a school environment. The vocabulary and skills developed in this preservice CoP should, if nurtured deliberately and effectively, help them move more smoothly into and contribute more meaningfully to future communities of pedagogical practice.

The nature of many preservice programs is that individual students move through a program of study in a prescribed way and complete the requirements of each course in much the same way as they did their general education courses. In programs that are organized into cohorts or in professional development schools, intentional or de facto CoPs emerge. My observations have been that where that happens the shared learning and construction of new knowledge happens in an ad hoc fashion. When that is the case the preservice teacher is learning from experience but they are not, as Tennant (1997) described, full participants in that world and in generating meaning.

Deliberate attention to the context of relationships and shared learning is needed if we want preservice teachers to participate in a CoP in which "the purpose is not to learn *from* talk as a substitute for legitimate peripheral participation; it is to learn *to* talk as a key to legitimate peripheral participation" (Lave & Wenger, 1991, pp. 108–109). The results of the pilot program described here suggest that using duoethnography at key points in the development of a preservice CoP could make that community more powerful but only if teacher educators and public school mentors help create relational environment in which to situate duoethnographic insights.

Embedding Duoethnography in Preservice Learning

The outcomes of the activities described in this chapter, while limited, showed enough potential pedagogical value to consider how duoethnography might be used in a systemic, developmental way throughout preservice education programs. It is with some hesitation that I make the recommendations that follow given the tendency for deeply reflective activities like developing a teaching philosophy or performance portfolio to become overly prescribed and superficial when made into curriculum requirements. This is especially true in an environment where accreditation pressures demand that activities be justified in terms of rubric-driven assessments. With that in mind, I recommend that if duoethnography is used in the ways described that it be used as an ungraded activity designed to provide readiness or context for future preservice learning.

Identifying Key Developmental Transitions

Baum and King (2006) found that when asked to discuss cultural influences on student behaviors, most preservice teachers were unable to do so, unless they themselves were members of a particular minority group. Engaging preservice teachers in a duoethnography that requires them to explore their own cultural contexts more deeply in juxtaposition with those of other students could begin to address that problem. This could be particularly successful if done at the beginning of a teacher education program since the results could provide a broader personal lens through which to perceive the rest of the curriculum and field experiences. The value of this approach is all the more obvious if we consider the importance of narrative in understanding teaching performance.

> A narrative perspective suggests that we invest most of our pre-performance energies in two areas. First, candidates would probably benefit from an orientation to classrooms as settings and as curriculum events. The main purpose here would be to give prospective teachers a language to begin talking about the elements that will constitute their experiences as performers in these environments. It would also prepare them to understand the fundamental management dilemmas they will encounter as they move into classroom practice. (Doyle & Carter, 2003, p. 135)

Similarly, duoethnographic conversations could be placed at one or two other crucial junctures of the program to prompt a more meaningful interpretation of coursework, field observations, or examination of how their own assumptions and skills have changed throughout the program. Some key developmental points, depending on the sequence and content of teacher preparation, might be after formal admission into the program, before beginning field experiences or student teaching, or before or after student teaching. The activity could also be placed within individual courses that are likely to cause more personal or professional dissonance than others, such as those dealing with multicultural or diversity issues. Regardless of where the strategy is used, if the research cited earlier is accurate, it is most important that duoethnography be used several times throughout the program in order to align with the evolutionary, developmental nature of changing teacher beliefs (Jacobs & Duhon-Sells, 1994; Stooksberry et al., 2009).

Fostering the Duoethnographic Context

In my own attempts at using duoethnography as a class activity I have come to see what other research has already established, that the climate in which such conversations take place is especially important. What that implies is that the environment in which the duoethnographies and follow-up discussions take place be safe and supportive. Beyond simple acceptance, the teacher educator should encourage and value the preservice teachers' insights and opinions. There should be no attempts at indoctrination, even if there are some dispositions and practices we hope the future teachers to obtain (Baum & King, 2006; Stookesbury et al.,

2009; Ünal, 2012). I believe the importance of environment was at play in the attempts at duoethnography described here.

There was a significant difference in climate between the small group of graduate preservice teachers in which there were no high stakes assessments and a more leisurely class setting in which conversation took place naturally and more in the manner of peers than in a teacher–student discussion. In contrast, the class in which the undergraduate students did their duoethnography was larger in number, early in the morning, and was laden with high stakes entrance to program requirements mandated by the department. The pace was also more rushed given the number of topics and activities to be completed. All of those factors conspired to create an environment that discouraged prolonged discussion of the process and results of the conversation. Based on other comments by students I am also sure that many students perceived the activity more as just another assignment than a reflective, developmental activity. Moreover, some noted the lack of consistent follow-up and meaningful use of the activity in class.

In the next iteration of duoethnography in my classes I believe the meaningfulness of the activity will be increased by making the activity more directed and interactive. This would mean making the duoethnography less of a research method and more a purposeful reflective tool. I believe that the nine prompts used with the undergraduate made the conversation too interview-like and will opt for the fewer but more open-ended and sequential prompts used with the graduate group. Similarly, the progressive approach used with the graduate students allowed for a slower but more interactive approach in which both the teacher and peers could react to and see models of conversation from the other participants (Knowles & Holt-Reynolds, 1991). Moreover, spreading the process over a longer period of time helped me to evaluate my own practice more effectively by giving me time to reflect on their responses, the progress of the duoethnography, and to share my own experiences with the method as a teaching tool for the preservice teachers (Baum & King, 2006).

Research on the relationship between life history and preservice conceptions of teaching consistently shows that past experiences are powerful influences on preservice development and that "researchers, teacher educators and preservice teachers need more insights into these beliefs in order to understand developmental tasks, that various contexts play a role in shaping beliefs and images, and that articulation of initial understanding is an important primary task" (Ebbs, 1997, p. 509). Duoethnography, with its combined emphasis on shared experiences, life history, and contextual knowing, could be uniquely qualified to accomplish each of those roles. It is important, though, that however it is used the duoethnography is not allowed to slide into yet another accreditation-driven benchmark or "key" assessment. What is needed now is more experimentation to determine the most meaningful way in which to use the process of duoethnography pedagogically while maintaining the integrity of the method itself.

References

Azevedo, R., & Cromley, J. G. (2004). Does training on self-regulated learning facilitate students' learning with hypermedia? *Journal of Educational Psychology, 96*, 523–535.

Bandura, A. (1977). *Social learning theory.* Upper Saddle River, NJ: Prentice Hall.

Beauchamp, C., & Thomas, L. (2009). Understanding teacher identity: An overview of issues in the literature and implications for teacher education. *Cambridge Journal of Education, 39*(2), 175–189.

Britzman, D. (1991). *Practice makes practice.* Albany, NY: State University of New York Press.

Buam, A. C., & King, M. A. (2006). Creating a climate of self-awareness in early childhood teacher preparation programs. *Early Childhood Education Journal, 33*(4), 217–222.

Bullough Jr., R. V., & Gitlin, A. D. (2001). *Becoming a student of teaching.* New York, NY: RoutledgeFalmer.

Calderhead, J., & Robson, M. (1991). Images of teaching: Student teachers' early conceptions of classroom practice. *Teaching and Teacher Education, 7*(1), 1–8.

Carter, K. (1993). The place of story in the study of teaching and teacher education. *Educational Researcher, 22*(1), 5–12.

Carter, K., & Doyle, W. (1996). Personal narrative and life history in learning to teach. In J. Sikula (Ed.), *Handbook of research on teacher education* (pp. 120–142). New York, NY: Simon & Schuster.

Chang, H., Ngunjiri, F. W., & Hernandez, K. C. (2013). *Collaborative autoethnography.* Walnut Creek, CA: Left Coast Press.

Clark, C. M. (1988). Asking the right questions about teacher preparation: Contributions of research on teaching thinking. *Educational Researcher, 17*(2), 5–12.

Cole, A. L. (1990). Personal theories of teaching: Development in the formative years. *Alberta Journal of Educational Research, 36*(3), 203–222.

Dewey, J. (1933). *How we think: A restatement of the relation of reflective thinking to the educative process* (1998 revised ed.). Boston, MA: Houghton Mifflin.

Doyle, W., & Carter, K. (2003). Narrative and learning to teach: Implications for teacher-education curriculum. *Journal of Curriculum Studies, 35*(2), 129–137.

Ebbs, C. (1997). Preservice teacher developmental tasks and life history. *Education, 117*(4), 598–603.

Edmunson, P. J. (1990). A normative look at the curriculum in teacher education. *Phi Delta Kappan, 71*, 717–722.

Eick, C., & Reed, C. (2001). What makes and inquiry-oriented science teacher? The influence of learning histories on student teacher role identity and practice. *Science Teacher Education, 86*(3), 401–416.

Furlong, C. (2013). The teacher I wish to be: Exploring the influence of life histories on student teacher idealised identities. *European Journal of Teacher Education, 36*(1), 68–83.

Green, T. (1971). *The activities of teaching*. New York, NY: McGraw-Hill.

Hammerness, K., Darling-Hammond, L., & Bransford, J. (2005). How teachers learn and develop. In L. Darling-Hammond & J. Bransford (Eds.), *Preparing teachers for a changing world: What teachers should learn and be able to do* (pp. 358–389). San Francisco, CA: Jossey-Bass.

Henderson, J. G. (2001). *Reflective teaching: Professional artistry through inquiry*. Upper Saddle River, NJ: Merrill Prentice Hall.

Hilson, R. (2008). One surprise after another. *Journal of Personality Assessment, 90*(3), 205–214.

Holt-Reynolds, D. (1992). Personal history-based beliefs as relevant prior knowledge in course work. *American Educational Research Journal, 29*(2), 325–349.

Jacobs, R. L., & Duhon-Sells, R. (1994). A strategy for maintaining the idealistic perceptions of preservice teachers. *Education, 115*(1), 87–96.

Kagan, D. M. (1992). Implication of research on teacher belief. *Educational Psychologist, 27*, 65–70.

Knowles, G., & Holt-Reynolds, D. (1991). Shaping pedagogies through personal histories in preservice teacher education. *Teachers College Record, 93*(1), 87–113.

Knowles, J. G. (1992). Models for understanding preservice and beginning teachers' biographies: Illustrations from case studies. In I. F. Goodson (Ed.), *Studying teachers' lives* (pp. 70–92). London, England: Falmer Press.

Lave, J., & Chaiklin, S. (Eds.). (1993). *Understanding practice: Perspectives on activity and context*. Cambridge, England: University of Cambridge Press.

Lave, J., & Wenger, E. (1991). *Situated Learning. Legitimate peripheral participation*. Cambridge, England: University of Cambridge Press.

Levin, B. B. (2003). *Case studies of teacher development*. Mahwah, NJ: Lawrence Erlbaum Associates.

Levison, A. B. (1974). The uses of philosophy and the problems of educators. In J. Park (Ed.), *Selected readings in the philosophy of education* (pp. 5–11). New York, NY: Macmillan.

Li, L. C., Grimshaw, J. M., Nielsen, C., Judd, M., Coyte, P. C., & Graham, I. D. (2009). Evolution of Wenger's concept of community of practice. *Implementation Science, 4*(11). doi:10.1186/1748-5908-4-11.

Lortie, D. C. (1975). *Schoolteacher: A sociological study*. Chicago, IL: University of Chicago Press.

McCulloch, A. W., Marshall, P. L., DeCuir-Gunby, J. T., & Caldwell, T. S. (2013). Math autobiographies: A window into teachers' identities as mathematics learners. *School Science & Mathematics, 113*(8), 380–389.

Mpungose, J. (2010). Constructing principals' professional identities through life stories: An exploration. *South African Journal of Education, 30*(4), 527–537.

Norris, J, & Sawyer, R. D. (2012). Toward a dialogic methodology. In J. Norris, R. Sawyer, & D. Lund (Eds.), *Duoethnography: Dialogic methods for social, health, and educational research* (pp. 9–39). Walnut Creek, CA: Left Coast Press.

Pajares, M. F. (1992). Teachers' beliefs and educational research: Cleaning up a messy construct. *Review of Educational Research, 3*, 307–332.

Peacock, M. (2001). Preservice ESL teachers' beliefs about second language learning: A longitudinal study. *System, 29*, 177–195.

Perry Jr., W. G. (1999). *Forms of ethical and intellectual development in the college years: A scheme*. San Francisco, CA: Jossey-Bass.

Polat, N. (2010). Pedagogical treatment and change in preservice teacher beliefs: An experimental study. *International Journal of Educational Research, 49*, 195–209.

Raths, J. (2001). Teachers' beliefs and teaching beliefs. *Early Childhood Research & Practice, 3*, 385–392.

Raths, J., & McAninch, A. C. (Eds.). (2003). *Teacher beliefs and classroom performance: The impact of teacher education*. Greenwich, CT: Information Age Publishing.

Sjølie, H., Karlsson, B., & Binder, P. (2013). Professionals' experiences of the relations between personal history and professional role. *Nursing Research and Practice, 2013*, 1–12.

Smith, M. K. (2003). Communities of practice. *The encyclopedia of informal education*. Retrieved from www.infed.org/biblio/communities_of_practice.htm

Stofflett, R. T., & Stoddart, T. (1994). The ability to understand and use conceptual change pedagogy as a function of prior learning experience. *Journal of Research in Science Teaching, 1*, 31–51.

Stooksberry, L. M., Schussler, D. L., & Bercaw, L. A. (2009). Conceptualizing dispositions: Intellectual, cultural and moral domains of teaching. *Teachers and Teaching: Theory and Practice, 15*(6), 719–736.

Tennant, M. (1997). *Psychology and adult learning*. London, England: Routledge.

Ünal, S. (2012). Evaluating the effect of self-awareness and communication techniques on nurses' assertiveness and self-esteem. *Contemporary Nurse, 43*(1), 90–98.

Vacc, N. N., & Bright, G. W. (1999). Elementary preservice teachers changing beliefs and instructional use of children's mathematical thinking. *Journal for Research in Mathematics Education, 30*(1), 89–110.

Weinstein, C. S. (1989). Teacher education students' preconceptions of teaching. *Journal of Teacher Education, 40*, 53–60.

Wenger, E. (1998). Communities of practice: Learning as a social system. *Systems Thinker*. Retrieved February 8, 2015, from http://www.co-i-l.com/coil/knowledge-garden/cop/lss.shtml

Wenger, E. (1999). *Communities of practice: Learning, meaning and identity*. New York, NY: Cambridge University Press.

Wisdom, J. (1963). *Problems of mind and matter*. Cambridge, UK: Cambridge University Press.

CHAPTER 5

Duoethnography as a Pedagogical Tool that Encourages Deep Reflection

Hilary Brown and Joe Barrett

As former teachers in the public sector, and, at present, teacher educators in a Faculty of Education, our past collaborative research was initiated through our genuine affinity for and love of teaching. Our casual discussions centered on the ways in which we each approached our teaching practice. We shared how and why we chose the content we wanted to teach and how we delivered our respective programs, and we discussed models and innovative teaching strategies beyond the traditional. As a result of our discussions, for our subsequent research we decided to infuse our teaching practice with an innovation approach. At the instructional level in our fields of expertise, Hilary being a Primary/Junior/Intermediate Foundational Methods instructor and Joe an Intermediate/Senior Health and Physical Education (HPE) instructor, we chose to implement duoethnography as a dialogic pedagogical tool and guide our teacher candidates through a deeply reflective process that interrogated both how methods students understood *diversity* and, second, how HPE students understood *mental health*. In short, we attempted to provide our teacher candidates with a tangible strategy to "get at" their understanding of diversity and mental

H. Brown (✉) • J. Barrett
Department of Teacher Education, Brock University,
St. Catharines, ON, Canada

J. Norris, *Theorizing Curriculum Studies, Teacher Education, and Research through Duoethnographic Pedagogy*,
DOI 10.1057/978-1-137-51745-6_5

health in a way that could potentially bring meaning to them personally, and, more importantly, make them learn how to negotiate their newly found understanding in their own teaching practice, with the recognition that all such knowledge are always "placeholders."

In order to guide our readers through the process of implementing a new approach we begin our chapter with background information on duoethnography in connection to how we used it as a pedagogical tool. Immediately we follow with an overview of the guiding principles or tenets of duoethnography that we felt complemented the depth of reflection we were aiming for with our teacher candidates. In order to solidify that connection, next we juxtaposed duoethnography as a pedagogical tool to Dewey's (1910/1933) notion of reflection as well as Larrivee's (2009) four levels of reflection. This in turn is followed by an in-depth description of the course assignment. From this point we shift from theory to practice and in the next section share our individual experiences implementing duoethnography as a pedagogical tool. We do so by honoring the voices of the teacher candidate as they began to think critically about themselves, their assumptions, and their teaching choices in direct relationship to undergoing a duoethnography. At the end of the chapter we come back together and share what we learned from our collaborative experiences.

Toward a Sense of Agency Using Duoethnography

Since duoethnography "challenges and potentially disrupts the metanarrative of self at the personal level by questioning held beliefs" (Norris & Sawyer, 2012, p. 15), we believed adapting this new research methodology and using it as a pedagogical tool that could also culminate as an assignment would evoke the critical and self-reflection necessary for the teacher candidates to experience the value in this beneficial lifelong skill.

Norris and Sawyer (2012) defined duoethnography as "a collaborative research methodology in which two or more researchers of difference juxtapose their life histories to provide multiple understandings of the world—duoethnography embraces the belief that meanings can be and often are transformed through the research act" (p. 9). This research methodology offers a lens toward the exploration of an experienced phenomenon and a concomitant study of the process through which individuals make meaning out a particular phenomenon (Norris & Sawyer, 2012). We were intrigued by its possible use as a pedagogical tool to explore both diversity and mental health as the experienced phenomena with the hope of "gaining critical awareness of [the student's] own narratives of experience through a dialogic process" (Norris & Sawyer, 2012, p. 3). Working with a critical partner, teacher candidates could uncover personal stories, memories, and experiences making explicit their assumptions, perspectives, and beliefs relating to diversity and mental health (Norris & Sawyer, 2012). We hoped that the employment of duoethnography as a pedagogical tool would lead teacher candidates to leave their teacher training with a greater sense of agency relating to both diversity and mental health instruction, while learning a unique way in which to support students. This exercise could also serve to lift the veil on teacher candidates' preconceived notions and existing judgments associated with the phenomena under study. Sawyer and Norris (2013) identified duoethnographies as "both a research process (form of data generation) and a research product (dissemination)" (p. 77) and we envisioned it as both a pedagogical process (evocation and analysis of experience) and teacher education product (greater sense of agency in relation to diversity and mental health instruction and ways in which to support students). The guiding principles or tenets of the duoethnographic process created a context for guiding teacher candidates to become reflective practitioners at all four levels of reflection: surface, pedagogical, critical, and the self. Our aspiration was that the latter two levels would be where our teacher candidates would spend most of their time. A discussion of the tenets follows.

The Guiding Principles or Tenets of Duoethnography

Norris and Sawyer (2012) list a growing number of emergent tenets (eight focused upon here) that make the duoethnographic process "distinct and strong" (p. 24). The first tenet draws on Pinar's (2004) notion of *currere* where the duoethnographer's life embodies a living, breathing curriculum. Our life histories become the site of the research. Within our personal curriculum we become engaged with ourselves through the other as we interrogate our past in light of the present with hope to transform our future. Second, duoethnographies are polyvocal and dialogic, meaning the voice of each participant is made explicit during the research process which leads to the third tenet of disrupting the metanarrative. The juxtaposition of the two stories or living curricula the duoethnographers have disclosed has an inherent third space (Bhabha, 1994) where the stories can potentially be restoried. This can only occur if the fourth tenet is present and that is when differences between the two participants have been clearly articulated. When differences are present this gives the duoethnographers an opportunity to question "meanings held about the past and invite reconceptualization" (Norris & Sawyer, 2012, p. 24) which is the fifth tenet. The sixth and seventh tenets flow from the notion that reconceptualization is necessary and that "universal truths are not sought" (p. 24) and that this reconceptualization is a "form of praxis where theory and practice converse" (p. 24). The final tenet, at the time of writing, reflects the negotiated space one enters when undergoing a duoethnography and the ethical stance which requires participants to be deliberately vigilant. These eight tenets are the guiding principles and dispositions that duoethnographers strive to adhere to in their research. They created a perfect fit for what we were attempting to achieve with our students and ourselves. Since our goal was to develop a practice that disrupts the status quo at the level of the teacher educator as well as of the teacher candidate, the seed took root for us to implement duoethnography as a pedagogical tool so that our students could have an opportunity to unearth any underlying prejudices they may hold while we do the same.

Duoethnography as a Pedagogical Tool that Encourages Deep Reflection

We adapted duoethnography as a research method and applied it as a pedagogical tool in the form of an instructional strategy where we had each teacher candidate explore, in conversation with another teacher candidate, the autobiographical and cultural events and influences that have shaped their beliefs, personality, and decisions (the implementation process within our own courses will be described later in the chapter within our individual stories). Within the duoethnographic experience, two texts were juxtaposed in order to create a new hybrid text residing within an interactive third space (Norris & Sawyer, 2012). The intention for creating this third space (Bhabha, 1994) was for the partners to challenge each other "to reflect on their own life in a deeper, more relational, and authentic manner" (Norris & Sawyer, 2012, p. 10). Hence, reflection is at the heart of the duoethnographic process.

Reflection

John Dewey (1910/1933) explored the concept of reflection. He considered it to be "an active and deliberative cognitive process which involves sequences of interconnected ideas that take into account underlying beliefs and knowledge" (Pedro, 2006, p. 130). He contrasted reflective thinking with "habits of thought that are unsystematic, lack evidence, rely on mistaken beliefs or assumptions, or mindlessly conform to tradition and authority" (Larrivee & Cooper, 2006, p. 2). With this in mind the process of the duoethnographic assignment is in direct alignment with Dewey's notion of what it means to be reflective. Dewey also believed that teachers who strive to be reflective share three common characteristics. First, they are open-minded and are willing to listen to more than one side of an issue, and give attention to alternative views. Second, reflective teachers are responsible and carefully consider the consequences of their actions, and, finally, they are wholehearted, meaning they are committed to seek every opportunity to learn (Dewey). These are the quintessential traits we wanted our teacher candidates to embrace when in conversation with their duoethnographic partner. The traits are in direct alignment with the tenets of the duoethnographic process. For example, being open-minded and willing to listen corresponds to the tenet of allowing the voice of each participant to be made explicit. In addition, being willing to listen to more than one side of an issue and giving attention to alternate views is consistent with the duoethnographic tenet that affirms the intention that the metanarrative will be disrupted. Our hope was that if our teacher candidates experienced an approach that required them to be open-minded, responsible, and wholehearted when in an explicit conversation with a classmate focused on a topic such as diversity and/or mental health, that if successful it could potentially "form the basis for not only considering alternatives, but also for taking action to continuously improve [his/her] practice throughout [his/her] teaching career" (Larrivee & Cooper, 2006, p. 2). Our desire for teacher candidates to take action further addresses the tenet that invites the duoethnographic partners to reconceptualize their present understanding of an issue in light of their partner's dialogic provocation. At the same time it gets at the notion that theory and practice need to come together for change to occur which is also a tenet of duoethnography. This level of engagement requires the participants to be willing to move from a surface and/or pedagogical reflection into a deeper level which encompasses both critical and self-reflection. In their duoethnographic partnerships, the negotiated space shaped by the ethical stance the partners arrived at infused by the inherent dialogic process (also tenets of duoethnography) encourages a deeper level of reflection than one person may arrive at on his/her own. In light of the connection between Dewey's notion of reflection and the tenets of duoethnography, we anticipated that the duoethnographic process could potentially guide teacher candidates into this depth of reflection.

Critical and Self-reflection

There are multiple levels of reflection. Larrivee (2009) presents a continuum of reflection from the simplest level, surface reflection, followed by pedagogical reflection proceeding to the higher-order levels of reflection of critical and self-reflection. Surface reflections tend to focus on what is working and what is not working in order to maintain order with little consideration of the value of these tasks. Pedagogical reflection tends to focus on the theory/practice divide: What teachers say they do in practice in relation to what they actually do in the classroom. Critical and self-reflection are considered higher-order levels due to the fact that one's biases, assumptions, values, as well as the consideration of the ethical implications of one's actions are brought to the surface in order to be interrogated, questioned, and challenged. Even though we taught all four levels of reflection our vision was to have our teacher candidates delve into forms of both critical and self-reflection. We did this by promoting an environment where awareness beyond the immediate was not only fostered but also encouraged as a normative function for a teacher candidate to possess. Through the duoethnographic project we guided our teacher candidates into these spaces and encouraged them to confront aspects of themselves that they perhaps had not considered before. We did this through the promotion of critical and self-reflection.

Critical reflection is the process by which people identify the assumptions governing their actions, locate the historical and cultural origins of the assumptions, question the meaning of assumptions, and develop alternate ways of acting (Cranton, 1996). At this level of reflection "teachers reflect on the moral and ethical implications and consequences of classroom practices on students." They "extend their considerations to issues beyond the classroom to include democratic ideals" (Larrivee & Cooper, 2006, p. 12). Through the process of critical reflection people come to interpret and create new knowledge and actions from their lived experiences. The intention is that they will change as a result of their newfound knowledge. Self-reflection on the other hand presumes that understanding oneself is a prerequisite to understanding others. It focuses on "examining how one's beliefs and values, expectations and assumptions, family imprinting, and cultural conditioning impact students and their learning" (Larrivee & Cooper, 2006, p. 13). While immersed in the duoethnographic process the teacher candidates needed to move between being critically reflective and self-reflective which allowed the creation of an interactive third space to open up where hybrid knowledge and understanding were enacted. Through this experience we hoped our teacher candidates would come to a better understanding of self in relation to diversity and mental health, and in turn find a way to disrupt teaching practices that were incongruent to their ontology and/or epistemology. Before we share the outline of the assignment some background information on duoethnography will help situate our study.

Duoethnography as Pedagogical Tool and Final Course Assignment

We adapted Rick Breault's (2012) duoethnography assignment to suit the topics of diversity and mental health issues. The following steps were both outlined in print and shared orally in our respective classes each week over the course of four class sessions. This is an abridged version.

- **Part 1: Initial Conversation (week 1–2)**

1. Find a conversation partner. Ideally, you should find someone with whom you share some important characteristic but someone who is also different from you in some significant way.
2. Devote one hour to a conversation about diversity/mental health. Record the conversation.
3. Transcribe the conversation. Take notes on what you think were important insights into your own teaching.

- **Part 2: Summarizing the Conversation (week 2–3)**

1. Write a summary of your own experiences as a student as it relates to diversity/mental health.

2. Write a similar summary for your conversation partner. This description will be your interpretation of what you heard in the conversation.
3. Be prepared to share your descriptions with each other and discuss how accurate and consistent your interpretations seem to be. Did you hear each other as you heard yourselves or as you intended to be heard by the other person?

- **Part 3: Searching Stories (week 4)**

After you have shared your interpretations, you need to search your stories for the impact they are having on your present preparation as a teacher and your future effectiveness in the classroom.

Distilling Meaning from Our Experiences with Duoethnography

In this section, we share our efforts to challenge the status quo—in this case, teacher candidates' biases, assumptions, and beliefs through dialogic explorations using duoethnography. First, we present each of our stories and, then, conclude with our shared and individual perspectives derived out of our interpretations of our learning about teaching using duoethnography.

Guiding Teachers to Become Critically Reflective (Hilary)

There are two main beliefs I have come to realize about my teaching and learning practice. First, I teach to disrupt the status quo that exists in education today specifically accountability and standardization whereby transmission of knowledge through testing has become the foci. In contrast, I choose to teach from a position of responsibility instead of accountability employing a holistic approach where balance, inclusion, and connection (Miller, 2007) are central features of my practice. "*Responsibility* and *accountability* point in different directions. We are *accountable* to a supervisor, someone above us in the hierarchy, but we are *responsible* for those below us, [hence] a sense of responsibility in teaching pushes us constantly to think about and promote the best interests of our students" (Noddings,

2012, p. 206). The notion of promoting the best interests of our teacher candidates leads me to the second theme I have come to realize about my teaching and learning practice, attending to the Other.

The Other is most often represented by "colonized, historically marginalized and oppressed groups" which fall under the "broad categories of non-Western, third world, developing, underdeveloped, First Nations, indigenous peoples, third world women, African American women and so on" (Chilisa, 2012, pp. 1–2). My worldview most definitely includes these broad categories but I also include people who have diverse learning needs in terms of learning styles, formal learning identifications, and physical disabilities, people whose socio-economic status is below the poverty line, people with mental health issues, and English language learners to name a few. I also teach acutely aware of language I use and the stories I share that highlight sexual orientation, gender issues, religion, ethnicity, and so forth.

Teaching to disrupt the status quo and honor the Other often challenges the assumptions of teacher candidates. With this in mind, it is important to note that I am open to having my preconceptions about teaching and learning challenged and disrupted at the same time as the teacher candidates. When I invited the teacher candidates to have a conversation with someone of difference during the duoethnography project they found themselves in unfamiliar territory. Simultaneously, I was working within unfamiliar territory since I had never attempted to implement duoethnography as an instructional strategy. As a result I viewed both the teacher candidates and myself as collaborators working through a disorienting dilemma where we were all experiencing feelings of discontent, restlessness, and insecurity but in slightly different ways.

Why Diversity?

I teach concurrent education teacher candidates in their fifth and final B.Ed. year. As a result of learning educational theory together as a cohort, a distinct group of learners with specific needs is organically shaped. The duoethnography assignment was developed both to evoke deep reflection and to challenge the teacher candidate's assumptions. I chose the topic of *diversity* for both theoretical and practical reasons. Theoretically, it was my hope that the consensus perspective would be challenged. In a consensus perspective education is seen as a means of providing skills training and knowledge transfer as well as basic societal values. The problem with the consensus perspective is that there is a refusal to acknowledge schools as sites where intergroup and class distinctions are reproduced or as arenas that do not serve the interest of less privileged members of society. Through an interrogative perspective, however, specifically critical theory, understanding the intersections of class, power, and privilege is critical to understanding how schools carry out their mandate and more specifically the role teachers play in that mandate. Second, duoethnography is a practical pedagogical tool that brings to the surface how class, power, and privilege underscore our actions. The juxtaposition of dialogic stories framed around the theoretical concept of diversity was a way to discover the teacher candidate's initial understanding of diversity. My hope was that this process would lead to a practical resolution whereby participants would become aware of their assumptions, biases, values, and beliefs and throughout the process negotiate with themselves how they were going to transform their preconceived notions in order to challenge the consensus perspective that drives education today.

My Experience with Duoethnography

I headed into this assignment with an optimistic mindset. I believed the topic of diversity was current, relevant, and interesting. I thought the concurrent students were going to immediately embrace this pedagogical tool and enjoy the process of deconstructing the concept diversity through critical and self-reflection. However, three challenges quickly emerged. First, even though I was aware that students took a course on diversity in their second year, I did not foresee that many students would come into the duoethnographic assignment believing they already *knew everything* there was to know about diversity. Second, I did not anticipate that they would resist talking to someone they did not know well. Finally, during the first session, in spite of the fact that the majority of students did find a conversational partner "who was different from him/her in some significant way," what emerged was that the Concurrent Program itself encouraged students to think the same way. One pair of students used the metaphor of the "funnel" to describe their experience in concurrent education. They determined that their backgrounds were fundamentally different but that the past four years had shaped their worldview and funneled their experiences through the philosophical underpinning of constructivism which encouraged them to adopt the same educational lens. My optimism was temporarily deflated but I persevered with my belief that we can all learn something even if the experience was not positive.

After the initial conversation, teacher candidates moved through the phases of the assignment from engaging in the accuracy and consistency of their partner's interpretations in comparison to their own interpretations, to the final phase where they distilled meaning from their reconstructed personal stories. In this phase they had the option to create their final piece through any mode that met their individual learning style. Some examples were poetry, short story, children's story, a formal paper, painting, collage, dance, digital media, sculpture, and so forth. The students chose a modality that brought meaning to their story while at the same time reflecting upon their future teaching and learning practice.

With Research and Ethics Board (REB) clearance granted at the conclusion of the assignment, I invited all 115 students to participate in a study sharing their duoethnographic experience. I inquired into whether they would allow me to use their course feedback form as well as their final duoethnography assignment as data. One hundred and four students consented, 8 declined, and 3 were absent when the invitation was extended. I was surprised by the number of students who allowed me to use their work as data since many students were initially irritated by the topic, the process of the assignment, as well as partnering with someone they did not know well. One student wrote:

> In the beginning I really didn't see the point of doing the assignment probably because I didn't know what I was supposed to do in the first place. After we got further into the assignment, I started to appreciate it and got to know a little bit about others, though it was a little awkward.

Another student mentioned that she "found this activity challenging at first because it was hard to open up with someone I had never met." This was a consistent theme throughout the data. However, some did embrace the opportunity:

> I found it very interesting how I was paired with someone I barely knew and our lived experiences were also different but our beliefs were very similar. I believe I have experienced some personal professional growth through small group discussions. It made me realize how important and useful collaboration among colleagues is!

Another theme that emerged was the process of reflection itself. Having an opportunity to reflect authentically at the level of self-reflection was new for a number of teacher candidates: "I learned how to dig deeper in my reflections—something I have always struggled with because I usually never go beyond the surface." Another woman stated, "Once I started doing the assignment I didn't realize how deep and personal it got for me. In the end I learned more about myself and my beliefs through this reflection." Being invited into a conversation with an unfamiliar partner moved the majority of the students out of their comfort zone. However, through the dialogic process they were respectfully encouraged to tap into their own living, breathing curriculum and use their life histories to examine why they believe what they believe. This example illustrates the depth of the first tenet whereby understanding the past can assist a person in transforming his/her future. Some students, however, commented on how trivial the first conversation was: "I found it difficult to have a deep conversation as most people were too polite or politically correct." However, she went on to offer suggestion for future improvement, "perhaps starting earlier to get used to your partner or allow us to switch and get multiple perspectives would improve this." Not all duoethnographic partnerships developed a healthy and trusting negotiated space as one of the tenets dictates, but perhaps starting earlier as this participant suggested will alleviate this concern. Finally, a consistent theme that emerged was that on the one hand the duoethnography lacked structure and explicit direction, which they found frustrating, yet, on the other hand, many participants concluded that feeling disoriented was worth it.

> I feel that this assignment could have been better explained. I understand that you did not want us to feel pushed into a certain direction. However, a little direction with clear instructions would have made this process more enjoyable for me. The duo project was an interesting task. When I got to the end, I began to understand how this could help me. I have had some difficult moments during this class. I feel that it helped me grow as a person. I have learned to adapt to situations that I am uncomfortable in. I have also learned to interact with differing teaching styles and philosophies.

Another woman stated that:

> At first it was uncomfortable to have vague(ish) instructions on assignments because I like direction. However, I think this strategy and the way you

> teach is actually how we should be taught (it got easier with time!) I hope to use this approach with my students—it definitely takes a confident teacher.

Both teacher candidates took away from the experience what they needed. This result is in alignment with the tenet that reconceptualization is necessary and both can and should move theory into conversation with practice. For me this was a win/win situation as both participants have grown in their own respective ways through the authentic implementation of a constructivist approach and one participant mentioned that she would be implementing this approach with her own students. Having an innovative pedagogical tool modeled created a disorienting dilemma. One woman summarized it in this manner:

> Your instructional strategy definitely took on the philosophy of constructivism as you fulfilled the role as guide in learning allowing us to take our own path in self-discovery and understanding. While I enjoy this strategy I could see the others were uncomfortable with this needing more structure. Like a classroom for my own students I think balance needs to be attained to allow all students to profit. The assignment was inventive and allowed those with good communicative skills to practice them but again this project (deconstructing diversity) has been over exercised.

The duoethnography assignment was not appreciated by a small percentage of the teacher candidates. One person wrote: "I did not feel the assignment was helpful in my growth. I felt the assignment was more of a time filler. Over the past 5 years we have talked about diversity so much and my opinions have not changed." This person did not come to a place where he wanted to reconceptualize his position on diversity. What became very clear as I read through the data was that no matter how hard I tried to meet the Concurrent students' unique learning needs, not all the teacher candidates transformed as a result of undergoing a duoethnography.

However, that being said, using duoethnography as a pedagogical tool definitely challenged the status quo and triggered many teacher candidates to think about their own biases and how they play out in their teaching practice. A range of responses were expressed from simply uncovering one's biases—*combining with another person to discuss diversity helped me to uncover more biases that I had,* which led to potentially acting upon those biases: *I am more aware of the choices I am making as a teacher as well as the biases and beliefs I have as a person that I take into my teaching.*

A deeper reflection illuminated how biases affect one's teaching:

> What was so powerful for me was that through the discussion I recognized some of my biases in relation to diversity AND the reasons I have developed those biases. I learned a lot about the environment I have grown up in how it influenced me and how I can change it. I feel I did experience growth through this course. It allowed me to reflect on my [teaching] block and what I did and why. I also learned a lot through other's experiences. I also feel I learned through the duoethnography: I learned about myself and my beliefs.

In the end some teacher candidates did arrive at a deeper understanding of diversity itself:

> The duo assignment actually encouraged me to self-reflect and express myself and explore these biases that I hold and whether I actually understood what diversity meant. At first I thought it would be simple to define the term diversity: however, it wasn't until the end of the activity I realized the complexity of the term and it was a challenge to define.

This type of response illustrates that the living curricula the duo partners disclosed did create a third space where their stories could potentially be restoried, where meanings from the past were challenged and space for reconceptualization could potentially occur. This was what I was hoping for when implementing this assignment with my teacher candidates. This fulfills yet another tenet behind the principles that guide duoethnography. Throughout the data analysis phase it became clear that the teacher candidates were pushed out of their comfort zone when faced with the task of deep reflection.

This type of interrogative assignment has established that as a teacher I have a *choice* of how I want to approach my teaching and learning practice simultaneously with my teacher candidates. By using duoethnography as a pedagogical tool I took a risk by inviting my teacher candidates to take an ethical stance and within a partnered negotiated space expose their vulnerabilities around the topic of diversity. They in turn either accepted or turned down the invitation to openly engage within the negotiated space. However, ultimately what became a central point of interest were my teacher candidates' future students. With them in mind I asked myself these questions. Do I want my teacher candidates to enter this profession with an open mind willing to listen to more than one side of an issue and give attention to alternative views? Do I want my teacher candidates to carefully consider the choices of their actions by interrogating their biases? And, finally, do I want them to remain wholehearted, committed to see every opportunity to learn? "Yes" is the unequivocal answer to all three questions. I know I strive to embody all three characteristics that are common to reflective teachers. But most importantly what I learned from the wide-ranging responses I received from the teacher candidates was that for the majority they, too, embody all three characteristics. What they need is to be continually pushed into uncomfortable spaces and learn in those moments that this is where meaningful knowledge is generated and, in turn, I will continue to push myself into those spaces as well.

Exploring Teacher Candidates' Notions of Mental Health (Joe)

As a new tenure track faculty member responsible for physical and health education teacher education (PHETE), I came to the faculty with a desire to provide co-constructed student-centered PHETE training. As with the experiences of Bullock and Christou (2009), Kitchen (2005), and Ritter (2007), I was entering into this phase of my teacher education career as a novice teacher educator and I approached this new direction with trepidation. In the midst of my developing pedagogy of PHETE, I was struggling with how to meaningfully situate the teaching of mental health education within my program. I knew I had a moral obligation to help teacher candidates find ways, in their teaching, to address the needs of students in the face of the emerging mental health challenges faced by children and youth in Canadian schools (Mental Health Commission of Canada, 2012).

Initially, my mental health education pedagogy largely focused on transmission of knowledge. This did not satisfy my overwhelming desire to help teacher candidates prepare for their teaching of and dealings with the estimated 1 in 5 Canadians under the age of 17 experiencing distress and impairment of function resulting from a mental health disorder (Waddell & Sheppard, 2002). In place of an innovative and student-centered pedagogy, I found myself enacting a pedagogy of PHETE where I used direct instruction to teach the signs, symptoms, and etiology of mental health while struggling with the contradiction between content, process of teaching, and desired learning outcomes (Russell, 2012). I was failing my students in this component of their PHETE training and I needed to change my practice.

The impetus for change was derived out of the review of my course evaluations. One evening while reading course evaluations I turned on the television and found myself passively interested in a program which featured an interview with Professor Temple Grandin from Colorado State University. She is a leading animal sciences professor and autism advocate. As the interview progressed, my passive interest gradually shifted toward active engagement and fascination with her message. In the interview, she clearly and concisely shared her perspectives on her own life's work and its impact on society. After years of struggle in mainstream society, it was evident that she knew who she was and, equally important, she knew how she had arrived at a clear conception of self—she was clear in her derived realizations about her life experiences and impact of those experiences on her life's work.

As the interview concluded, I picked up the course evaluations and read through teacher candidates' reflections on their PHETE training. I found numerous expressions of concern regarding preparedness relating to the teaching of mental health education in schools. One teacher candidate indicated:

> I thought mental health was very much looked at as a stigma in society and was swept under the rug because it was not something that should ever be talked about. If you have a mental illness you have a problem. I believed that the teaching of mental health was very much ignored and feared by many teachers. I feel this correlates with the lack of education I have had on the topic. I never had any sort of discussion on mental health in either elementary school or high school, and I have discussed it very minimally in university. I feel as though even with our teacher's college training we receive little or no support on how to deal with mental illness in the classroom or even discuss what it really is and what it means.

I realized that my current course structure was leaving teacher candidates to deal with a disconnection that would neither be remedied nor addressed prior to the conclusion of their PHETE training. They were left on their own to confront a rather narrow and reactive view toward student mental health. I found myself interpreting the teacher candidate reflections with a lens toward improving teacher candidates' sense of agency with mental health education and student support (Marcel, 2003). I chose to operationalize a sense of agency, from a teacher education standpoint, as a teacher candidates' ability to take action, be effective, understand his/her conception of self, and demonstrate competence utilizing co-constructed student-centered pedagogy. In the face of stigmas attached to mental illness and the lack of awareness of how to recognize and support students with mental health challenges (Barrett & Dewar, n.d.; Gowers et al., 2004; Walter, Gouze, & Lim, 2006) some of my students were not embarking on a teaching career able to interpret their roles and responsibilities associated with student mental health education. This teacher candidate wrote:

> Mental health. What a loaded term. When I think of mental health I am immediately drawn to personal family experiences and I often become somewhat emotional or angry when thinking about it. Because I do not suffer from a mental health issue, it is very hard for me to try to put myself in student's shoe that has a mental illness. I am an extremely black and white person and I find it hard to relate to people that suffer from mental health issues.

That evening I became consumed with the notion that I could do something more to ensure a sense of agency that would lead to the enactment of (a) teaching of mental health education curricula, (b) supporting of student mental health and wellness, and (c) fostering of nurturing learning environment for all students. I found myself enveloped and painfully self-aware of this nodal moment (Bullough & Pinnegar, 2001). I was moving between feelings of helplessness, fascination, and a desire to better understand or explore how I might help my students achieve a sense of agency with mental health education instruction and student support. Inspired by Dr. Grandin and the honesty present in my students' course evaluation statements, I made the decision to have my future teacher candidates begin with an exploration of their own journey and experiences with mental health. According to Grandin (2011), "The best thing a parent of a newly diagnosed (autistic) child can do is to watch their child, without preconceived notions or judgments, and learn how the child functions, acts, and reacts to his or her own world" (p. 5).

Dr. Grandin's words would serve as a metaphor for my learning to teach PHETE teacher candidates about how to explore their own notions, underlying prejudices, and understandings of mental health using duoethnography. While traditionally defined as a research methodology, I believed that duoethnography as a pedagogical tool could provide teacher candidates with an approach to the juxtaposition of life stories and histories in relation to mental health (Norris & Sawyer, 2012). I was also hoping that through teacher candidates' duoethnographic explorations of mental health that they would help each other find their way to reconceptualized and transformed notions of mental health education teaching and support of students afflicted by mental health disorders.

In the Beginning There Was Reflection

In preparation for our duoethnographic exploration of mental health, I turned to an existing body of work which identified a clear and evidence-based need to help teacher candidates address personal biography, their existing beliefs, values, and intentions derived from their own personal experiences, where failing to do so may lead to a rejection of messages and lessons learned through PHETE experiences (Matanin & Collier, 2003; Morgan, 2008; Placek et al., 1995). I kept coming back to the experiences of Dr. Grandin. Through her life struggles, the process that she had moved through was evolutionary and at its root reflective. I, then, considered the work of Lyons (1998) who offered, "the development of reflection is considered not simply as change, but as the evolution and integration of more complex ways (or processes) of engaging in critical examination of one's teaching practices" (p. 115). I felt strongly that the core tenets of duoethnography could provide the theoretical underpinnings necessary for me to help to develop a reflective student-centered experience that emphasized a "reconstruction or reorganization of experience which adds to the meaning of experience, and which increases [one's] ability to direct the course of the subsequent experience" (Dewey, 1944, p. 74). I, like Hilary, had no prior experience with the implementation of duoethnography as a part of my pedagogy of PHETE. I leaned into the uncertainty, with my students. Together, we confronted both a challenging topic, mental health, and the challenge of using duoethnography processes in teacher education practice.

Teacher Candidates as Duoethnographers

PHETE candidates began a duoethnographic assignment after they had completed one of their three scheduled practicum placements. Before introducing the assignment, I wanted them to have had a field experience in K-12 schools that would offer a reference point for the realities faced by current secondary students in an HPE context. When introducing the assignment, teacher candidates were asked to find a partner and be prepared to share with their colleagues how and why the two individuals comprising the dyad were fundamentally different. Initially, there was a flurry of questions. What do you mean by different? How different do we have to be? Do we have to be different in a certain number of ways?

I decided against providing any further guidance and I encouraged them to go into the exercise free of any external constraints that I might place on the exercise. I watched as teacher candidates moved freely through the room engaging in sometimes brief and other times extended conversations. From this initial exercise, teacher candidates were creating their "duo" that would provide the context for their exploration of mental health. As the facilitator of learning in this early phase of the duoethnographic exploration, I was pleasantly surprised by the thoughtfulness and understandings about what made each individual in the "duo" fundamentally different. In most instances, the differences were deep and layered taking into account, demographic factors, interests, and epistemological differences. Free of my constraints, they engaged and were ready to learn where this initial exercise might take them. I introduced the teacher candidates to the methodology of duoethnography as previously outlined in this chapter.

At the conclusion of this exploration of duoethnography as pedagogy, I was drawn back to the words of Bullough and Pinnegar (2001) positioning that the "self-study researcher has an ineluctable obligation to seek to improve the learning situation not only for the self but for the other" (p. 17). Was I able to improve PHETE candidates' sense of agency relating to mental health through the use of a duoethnography as a pedagogical tool? All 22 of my PHETE candidates provided consent for the use of their completed assignments and course feedback forms as data. The data collected were analyzed using line-by-line open coding to determine emerging themes (Strauss & Corbin, 1998). After the entire data set was reviewed multiple times, the responses were categorized into emergent themes. Although not the main focus of the study, the student data were included to underpin and inform my learning to teach PHETE teacher candidates about how to explore their own notions, underlying prejudices, and understandings of mental health using duoethnography. Specifically, PHETE candidates' dialogues were included to elucidate (a) the perceived value, if any, PHETE candidates placed on the use of duoethnography as a pedagogical tool, and (b) the extent to which the assignment impacted their sense of agency relating to mental health instruction and support. With respect to the process, one student wrote:

> Overall, I really enjoyed the whole assignment. Working with a partner in a safe environment really allowed me to open up about past experiences.

Another student offered:

> Duoethnography and my partner made me more aware of how my views and perceptions are interpreted by others … it was scary. Everyone has their own story but rarely are we provided with an opportunity to analyze how those stories influence our behaviours.

Core to the tenets, some of my teacher candidates were able to share freely and safely, "recalling meaningful events and reading personal beliefs within a playful yet disciplined dialogic frame—part of the currere and subsequently the duoethnography" (Sawyer & Norris, 2013, p.15).

Teacher candidates also noted that they could see themselves using this instructional approach with their own secondary students:

> I learned so much about myself. I will most likely use this strategy with my own secondary students.

This practice-focused sentiment was echoed by a peer who noted:

> I see tremendous value in its use in school settings. I can see this being a valuable tool to use for in-service teacher training. Many of the teachers I worked with on practicum would benefit from an exploration of their biases, and perspectives in a low pressure conversational manner.

Finally, one candidate shared the following:

> Using duoethnography to explore this topic could help secondary students see that there are others who have the same kinds of thoughts about life, stress, and health. Using something like this could better equip students to emotionally handle the ups and downs in life and continue on. If you were doing this again, I would suggest you create large duo groupings so that we can hear more from others. Keep the process the same but allow me to pair up with more of my colleagues. I would have benefited from reflecting upon multiple perspectives.

Using duoethnography resulted in a bridging of theory and practice for many of the teacher candidates—an unexpected, yet, desirable outcome.

Teacher candidates reported on ways in which duoethnography could (a) be improved, (b) support student learning and, (b) support in-service teacher professional development. Grounded on the tenets, our duoethnography design led to a teacher candidates' recognition that "its value and meaning are found in its contribution to the improvement of life experience" (Sawyer & Norris, 2013, p.33).

Finally, I also wanted to determine whether PHETE candidates' sense of agency relating to mental health instruction and student support were impacted through the use of this duoethnographic exploration of mental health. One student wrote:

> When I am confused and unsure about something (mental illness) I am more likely to pretend it isn't there. If I don't know how to handle a situation I am very unlikely to enter it as I would fear doing the wrong thing. This could be detrimental in the classroom, as something will need to be done for these students with mental illness. I will get to know my students on a more personal level and therefore am more likely to be the one they will go to when wanting to discuss these issues. I therefore need to be ready and not just push them aside or pawn them off on someone else because I now recognize that I might be the only person they feel comfortable talking with.

Nine of the 22 PHETE candidates made specific reference to growth and change in perspective. One PHETE candidate stated:

> Overall, this activity has really helped me grow as an educator. I've never really taken the time to sit down and review how I feel about mental illness. It has allowed me to point out my biases and taught me that I need to change if I truly want to be an effective teacher for my students. I have discovered that I not only lack education about the topic but also lack real world exposure to those suffering from mental illness. This activity has taught me that I need to be more aware of my students' feelings and change my own beliefs about mental illness in order to better serve my students.

Another student shared the following:

> To be honest this exercise has been completely eye opening for me. I did not realize how much my personal family life has had an impact on how I feel about mental health. I feel as though I have a lot of bias when it comes to mental health because I have watched two different people that I love go through it.

In a similar fashion to Hilary's students, self-reflexive engagement led to the creation of a third space and more importantly, for many, led to change. True to the tenets, many were able to find their way to safe and comfortable conversational spaces despite their differences. In those experiences, it was evident that teacher candidates were engaging in communal *yet critical conversations* with a focus on the self through the "other" deconstructing meanings held in their own past and still inviting reconstruction of meaning and stories (Sawyer & Norris, 2013). As in the case of Hilary's students, some partnerships could not overcome their differences and, as a result, were frustrated with the assignment openly questioning the purpose and value associated with the exploration. I left the assignment questioning on two fronts. First, were the differences between the candidates acting as barriers to their engagement in currere, a core tenet underpinning their duoethnography? And last, were those frustrated with the process "ready" for an immersive self-reflexive and dialogic exploration centered around a challenging topic such as mental health? I would suggest that despite the challenges faced in the present exploration, the value associated with the exposure and experience still needs to be realized and this may require further study by teacher education faculty choosing to utilize duoethnography as a pedagogical tool in teacher education practice.

Conclusion

During our collaborative research project, our discussions consistently arrived at the same intersection and that is our communal commitment to providing the best teaching and learning practice possible. Keeping in mind that in the academy one's teaching practice is generally not as well respected as one's research agenda, this reality added an unwavering tension in our ongoing dialogue. As a result of our ontological as well as epistemological commitment to teaching and learning, we were both willing to take risks to continually improve our practice. As teacher educators we find it *necessary* to continue to hone our craft so that our teacher candidates experience best practices in action. It is our hope that they, too, will embrace the notion of how important it is to take risks by trying new techniques in their own classrooms. In our roles as teacher educators this collaborative study helped us to name what we attempt to do every time we step into a classroom. By naming ourselves as risk takers we acknowledge that this path is not for everyone but leading our teacher candidates through a disorienting dilemma was the only plausible way to get at these important issues that are pervasive in teacher education today.

Our duoethnographic explorations have provided us with a way to support one another through the implementation of a new pedagogical tool in order to improve our teaching and learning practice. Implicit in our ambition to improve our teaching and learning practice is the notion that this will also promote the same ambition in our teacher candidates. Throughout the implementation of the duoethnography assignment, many teacher candidates began to question their assumptions which invited them to move to the level of self-reflection. This reaches to the heart of teaching and learning when one is able to examine how one's beliefs, values, expectations, family imprinting, and cultural conditioning impact students and their learning (Larrivee & Cooper, 2006). We witnessed students engaged, at times, in the struggle of uncovering some not so complimentary revelations about their lives while we uncovered some of our own. While in the exploration of the self, most of the teacher candidates, as evidenced by their written feedback forms critiquing the duoethnography assignment, their final assignments, and overall course evaluations, were able to identify their own biases and assumptions related to diversity and mental health. From this awareness the students came to a newfound consideration of how their biases and assumptions could potentially negatively or positively influence others, more specifically their future students. From this new understanding many wanted to develop alternate ways of acting. They used action-oriented language to express how they were going to interact with others differently. For Joe, this result was different from previous teaching encounters. He had no previous evidence of student growth or pedagogical competence associated with mental health education. Hilary, on the other hand, had had similar results when using other constructivist teaching strategies (see Brown, 2012).

Dewey (1910/1933) believed that for people to be reflective they needed to be open-minded and willing to listen to more than one side of an issue, while giving attention to alternative views. He also believed they should carefully consider the consequences of their actions and ultimately he viewed reflective teachers as wholehearted, meaning they were committed to seek every opportunity to learn (Dewey). These are the traits we promoted and fostered throughout the duoethnographic assignment. Near the end of the assignment we eventually observed these traits in our teacher candidates as they maneuvered through the challenging task of both critical and self-reflection

While engaged in the duoethnographic assignment, we, too, struggled alongside our students. By stepping into the unknown and implementing an experimental pedagogical tool we too experienced a disorienting dilemma which we had to navigate. By diligently working through the assignment, we have come to believe that duoethnography can serve well as a pedagogical tool. It was a risk was worth taking. Our students valued the experience with many indicating that they would choose to use duoethnography with their own students in their future education classes. We, too, will continue to use it in our classes. It is a pedagogical tool that can be used to purposefully deconstruct one's personal biography contextualized around the exploration of a phenomenon such as diversity and mental health but other topics could be explored as well. Duoethnography in this context provided a defined path to meaningful reflection and action for both our teacher candidates and our selves. Moreover, our collaboration provided us with the occasion to deconstruct duoethnographic explorations in our respective classes, but also reconstruct our own teaching and learning practice in a more meaningful and fulfilled manner. We believe we must continue to offer opportunities for our teacher candidates to do the same.

References

Bhabha, H. K. (1994). *The location of culture.* New York: Routledge.

Breault, R. (2012). *Duoethnography with entering preservice teachers.* Paper presented at the International Congress of Qualitative Inquiry, University of Illinois at Urbana-Champaign.

Brown, H. (2012). In order to be you have to be: Modeling a constructivist approach for teacher candidates. *Brock Education, 21*(2), 36–52.

Bullock, S. M., & Christou, T. (2009). Exploring the radical middle between theory and practice: A collaborative self-study of beginning teacher educators. *Studying Teacher Education, 5*(1), 75–88.

Bullough, R. V., & Pinnegar, S. (2001). Guidelines for quality in autobiographical forms of self-study research. *Educational Researcher, 30*(3), 13–21.

Chilisa, B. (2012). *Indigenous research methodologies.* Los Angeles, CA: Sage.

Cranton, P. (1996). *Professional development as transformative learning: New perspectives for teachers of adults.* San Francisco, CA: Jossey-Bass.

Dewey, J. (1910/1933). *How we think: A restatement of the relation of reflective thinking to the educative process.* Lexington, MA: Heath.

Dewey, J. (1944). *Democracy and education.* New York: Free Press.

Gowers, S., Thomas, S., & Deeley, S. (2004). Can primary schools contribute effectively to tier I child mental health services? *Clinical Child Psychology and Psychiatry, 9*(3), 419–425.

Grandin, T. (2011). *The way I see it: A personal look at autism & asperger's.* Arlington, TX: Future Horizons.

Kitchen, J. (2005). Conveying respect and empathy: Becoming a relational teacher educator. *Studying Teacher Education, 1*(2), 194–207.

Larrivee, B. (2009). *Authentic classroom management: Creating a learning community and building reflective practice.* Upper Saddle River, NJ: Pearson.

Larrivee, B., & Cooper, J. M. (2006). *An educator's guide to teacher reflection.* Boston, MA: Cengage Learning.

Lyons, N. (1998). Reflection in teaching: Can it be developmental. *Teacher Education Quarterly, 25,* 115–127.

Marcel, A. J. (2003). The sense of agency: Awareness and ownership of action. In J. Roessler & N. Eilan (Eds.), *Agency and self-awareness* (pp. 48–93). Oxford: Oxford University Press.

Matanin, M., & Collier, C. (2003). Longitudinal analysis of preservice teachers' beliefs about teaching physical education. *Journal of Teaching in Physical Education, 22,* 153–168.

Mental Health Commission of Canada. (2012). *Changing directions, changing lives: The mental health strategy for Canada.* Calgary, AB: Author.

Miller, J. P. (2007). *The holistic curriculum* (2nd ed.). Toronto, ON: University of Toronto Press.

Morgan, P. (2008). Teacher perceptions of physical education in the primary school: Attitudes, values and curriculum preferences. *Physical Educator, 65,* 46–56.

Noddings, N. (2012). *Philosophy of education* (3rd ed.). Philadelphia, PA: Westview Press.

Norris, J., & Sawyer, R. D. (2012). Toward a dialogic methodology. In J. Norris, D. S. Sawyer, & D. Lund (Eds.), *Duoethnography: Dialogic methods for social, health, and educational research.* Walnut Creek, CA: Left Coast Press.

Pedro, J. (2006). Taking reflection into the real world of teaching. *Kappa Delta Pi Record, 42*(3), 129–132.

Pinar, W. F. (2004). *What is curriculum theory?* Mahwah, NJ: Lawrence Erlbaum Associates.

Placek, J. H., Dodds, P., Doolittle, S. A., Portman, P. A., Ratliffe, T. A., & Pinkham, K. M. (1995). Teaching recruits' physical education backgrounds and beliefs about purposes for their subject matter. *Journal of Teaching in Physical Education, 14,* 246–261.

Russell, T. (2012). Science teacher education, self-study of teacher education practices, and the reflective turn. In S. M. Bullock & T. Russell (Eds.), *Self-study, science teaching, and science teacher education.* Dordrecht, The Netherlands: Springer.

Ritter, J. K. (2007). Forging a pedagogy of teacher education: The challenges of moving from classroom teacher to teacher educator. *Studying Teacher Education, 3*(1), 5–22.

Sawyer, R., & Norris, J. (2013). Understanding qualitative research: Duoethnography. New York: Oxford University Press.

Strauss, C., & Corbin, J. (1998). *Basics of qualitative research: Techniques and procedures for developing grounded theory*. Thousand Oaks, CA: Sage.

Waddell, C., & Shepherd, C. (2002). *Prevalence of mental disorders in children and youth*. Research update prepared for the British Columbia Ministry of Children and Family Development, University of British Columbia, Vancouver, BC.

Walter, H. J., Gouze, K., & Lim, K. G. (2006). Teachers' beliefs about mental health needs in inner city elementary schools. *Journal of the American Academy of Child & Adolescent Psychiatry, 45*(1), 61–68.

CHAPTER 6

Exploring Duoethnography in Graduate Research Courses

Darren E. Lund, Kimberley Holmes, Aubrey Hanson, Kathleen Sitter, David Scott, and Kari Grain

Introduction

This chapter explores the rich potential of duoethnography as a research methodology in the social sciences and humanities, with particular attention to its dialogic and pedagogic features that make it an ideal means of exploration in a range of graduate research courses. I have enjoyed a decade of experience working with the approach, and have published and participated in a number of early duoethnographies with a range of peers, students, and colleagues. The approach has informed my university teaching, and it has been particularly salient in the teaching of collaborative and participatory research methods. Students undertaking graduate and doctoral-level study of a range of qualitative research methods have found this approach refreshing and groundbreaking in many specific ways.

D.E. Lund (✉) • K. Holmes • A. Hanson • D. Scott
University of Calgary, Calgary, AB, Canada

K. Sitter
Memorial University of Newfoundland and Labrador, St. John's, NL, Canada

K. Grain
University of British Columbia, Vancouver, BC, Canada

J. Norris, *Theorizing Curriculum Studies, Teacher Education, and Research through Duoethnographic Pedagogy*,
DOI 10.1057/978-1-137-51745-6_6

The dialogic approach encourages deliberate self-reflection among students, and a critical examination of the beliefs and values underlying their practice. Further, there now exists a growing body of research and theory, including the seminal writings by the founders of this approach (Norris, 2008; Sawyer & Norris, 2013), and an edited collection that students can consult to feed their own understandings and articulations of this new lens for inquiry (Norris, Sawyer, & Lund, 2012). In this chapter I draw upon accounts of this work coming alive in the graduate research courses and seminars that I taught, through the invited voices of students who offer encouragement for more scholars to engage and extend duoethnography in their university classes. This approach also signals a dialogic and democratic way to resist and counter some of the current dehumanizing aspects of university life.

Resisting an Increasingly Neoliberal Academy

There is a disquieting trend in the academy that has had the effect of inhibiting authentic dialogue and intellectual inquiry, and is more about creating market-driven models of education that place profit, performance, and bureaucratic compliance above deep intellectual and ethical engagement (Giroux, 2010; Panayotidis, Lund, Towers, & Smits, 2016; Ritzer, 2014). Within this framework, students are seen as consumers, and faculties are tasked with maximizing profits while providing a service for money. As Jubas and Seidel (2014) describe current conditions in universities, "economic viability and purpose replace older scholarly values, including intellectual rigor, human development, personal fulfillment, and social justice. Rhetoric of commerce and industry infiltrates academic discussions, whether by intention or by accident" (p. 17). This tendency toward capitalist models of universities—as sites of standardized information delivery, testing, and credential granting—has also meant the devaluing of conversation, deep reflection, ethical collaboration, and authentic intellectual engagement.

Engaging in authentic dialogue with others—as afforded by duoethnography—is a richly rewarding endeavor that fosters a shared experience, one that is based on openness to others. As Freire (1998) explains it,

> To live in openness toward/others and to have an open-ended curiosity toward life and its challenges is essential to educational practice. To live this openness toward others respectfully and, from time to time, when

> opportune, critically reflect on this openness ought to be an essential part of the adventure of teaching. The ethical, political, and pedagogical basis of this openness confers on the dialogue that it makes possible a singular richness and a beauty. (pp. 120–121)

I argue that such deep-seated beliefs require significant personal courage and a willingness to be more vulnerable than with more typically "neutral" intellectual and research activities.

In contrast to encouraging dialogue and collaboration, the new university focuses on top-down models of governance that tend to reduce individual efficacy in favor of larger-scale impersonal institutional measures of effectiveness and success. Giroux (2011) characterizes this movement as part of "casino capitalism," and describes its effect on universities as tending to "deaden the imagination by defining and framing classroom experiences through a lethal mix of instrumental values, cost-benefit analyses, test-based accountability schemes, and high-stakes testing regimes" (p. 114). Further, our new education models have inhibited "those spaces and pedagogical practices that provide the conditions for students to think critically, value their own voices, mobilize their curiosity, engage in shared learning … necessary for fostering a real democracy and taking responsibility for sustaining it" (p. 114). Within this context, individualism and competition are rewarded. The very notion of collaborative, dialogic approaches has been tainted by a neoliberal discourse into merely describing a way to improve a faculty member's success with securing large competitive research grants; as Glaser (2015) notes, "ultimately, resistance is impossible without collective solidarity: compliance is a facet of isolation. While 'collaboration' has become a buzzword of the grant bid, structural possibilities for cross-university cooperation remain woefully limited" (para. 10). I envision the role of highly collaborative and dialogic approaches such as duoethnography as providing a specific possibility for resistance, a glimmer of hope for shaping a better future for those of us in the academy and beyond.

Early Duoethnographic Studies

In the past decade since first learning about duoethnography at a curriculum conference on the west coast of Canada (Norris & Sawyer, 2005), I have been fortunate to spend a lot of time with the method and its creators. This time has included some very fruitful conversations with

Rick and Joe, and with a number of other scholars who have adopted this dialogic mode of inquiry in their academic and aesthetic work. Each year, more people learn about this approach, and the growing cadre of engaged scholars continues to add great richness to the constant growth and advancement of the field. At conferences on educational research, qualitative methodology, critical pedagogy, and curriculum studies, people gather to talk about how they conceptualize, plan, and use the method in their work. The constant push and pull of debate, the crossing of boundaries in our sense of identity as people and as researchers, and the robust discussions about tenets of the approach all contribute to a rich discourse on innovative forms of ethnographic research. Meaningful dialogues with colleagues, reviewing each others' writing, and sharing our findings at conferences are all lovely additional benefits of bringing a vibrant new methodology into being. I was honored to play an editorial role in the production of one of the collaborative volumes featuring an exciting range of examples of duoethnography (Norris et al., 2012). In each instance, my understandings of the method have been filtered through the lens of my own experimentation with the approach in collaborations with colleagues and graduate students.

Introducing Graduate Students to Duoethnography

Over the years I have regularly shared examples of duoethnography as part of my teaching at the university, and in talks and guest lectures with undergraduate, graduate, and doctoral students, as a way of opening up possibilities to consider emerging methodologies. I have given talks about duoethnography to graduate students in social work, education, nursing, medicine, sociology, and law. I have also encouraged students to take up the approach for course assignments and tentative field experiences with research methodology. For example, graduate and doctoral courses I have taught over the years have included Qualitative Research Methods, Participatory Methods in Education, and Ethnographic Research Approaches, and in each course I have included an assignment that encourages students to undertake an independent research project that may include either observation or interview. As part of the course we cover duoethnography as one of the methodologies, often with a guest lecture from a student or colleague who has used the approach. Just this past semester in an education doctoral seminar with school and school district leaders, I invited three guest lecturers over the semester who each shared their experiences with dialogic methods, including duoethnography. All three of them had published their work in scholarly journals and books, and all were very articulate in sharing both the joys and challenges of their collaborative meaning-making through this approach. My doctoral students were eager to ask them specific questions in class about undertaking this work, including on ethical considerations, vulnerabilities, boundaries and self-disclosure, emotionality, editing and revising, and publishing, among other topics.

A number of students have chosen to engage in a duoethnographic dialogue as part of their coursework, and some have also undertaken them outside of the course for their own interest, to assess the relevance to their own theses or dissertation research programs, or for generating insights on topics of interest to them. One of my assignments involved undertaking field work using a specific approach, and each semester, some students choose duoethnography. The intention is not to undertake research that they will publish or disseminate, but to explore their comfort with dialogic meaning-making, and to check the fit of an approach they have read about. Their understandings of methods and methodology become so much deeper when they actually get to jump into the field themselves in this tangible way, bringing their readings into the light of their lived experiences with this approach. Students sometimes tell me that they get the impression when reading academic literature that everything significant has already been invented or discovered, and that the widely known research approaches we know and use seem like a finite and closed set of options. Learning about a new and exciting form of ethnography that builds on autoethnography seems to fracture this way of thinking for graduate students; it indicates to them that there remains much more to learn, and that they can perhaps discover a new approach—or application of an approach—through their own research.

Even more significantly, the focus of duoethnography on dialogue and narrative, the complete engagement of two people on a topic, and the inclusion of deeply personal biographies on a curriculum of learning about an issue can be a very humanizing endeavor. Students report that this dialogic approach, undertaken in concert with another, has a way of fostering deeper reflexivity and self-critical understandings—as well as insights about the chosen research topic at hand—all of which are essential as precursors to undertaking any qualitative or interpretive research.

The experiences remind them that engaging in dialogic forms of research offers human connection and a sense of care for the other that too often seems missing in the scholarly world, and, many would argue, in the world at large. Ayers (2001) highlighted the tremendous power and excitement of using dialogue in education, writing that "while in every dialogue there are mistakes, misperceptions, struggle, and emotion, it is the disequilibrium of dialogue that leads to exploration, discovery, and change" (p. 138). Indeed, it is an admittedly messy but highly democratizing effort. Dialogue, according to Ayers,

> is undertaken with the serious intention of engaging others. This means we speak with the possibility of being heard, and listen with the possibility of being changed. ... We commit to questioning, exploring, inquiring, paying attention, going deeper. ... All of this is based on an unshakable faith in human beings. (p. 139)

It is through the shared engagement, the caring about others, and the genuine effort to understand another perspective on an issue of importance to the educative endeavor that the significance of adopting dialogic approaches such as duoethnography is elevated. As Pauline Sameshima (2013) writes in her essay review of the two major texts (Norris et al., 2012; Sawyer & Norris, 2013) that have been published on duoethnography to date:

> The reader of a duoethnographic study engages in a complicit conversational *currere* with the texts and is challenged to name and negotiate discursive contradictions which in turn encourage deeper questioning. ... [These two books] create their own dialogue in support of politically engaged, socially complex and cosmopolitan, and inherently democratic curriculum theory. Duoethnography pushes our field forward by legitimizing a space to revive repressed, embodied knowing, challenging our socially constructed frameworks. (p. 16)

It is this shared extension of a larger, educational democratic project that enriches both the participants and the social world in which it takes place.

Former students of mine from various graduate courses and commitments over the past few years have contributed the accounts below. When invited, they each offered these thoughts on their experiences with duoethnography, and granted permission for their inclusion here. Rather than offering critique and analysis of their narratives, I prefer to let them speak on their own terms as a compelling testimonial to their particular research and learning experiences, with some summary comments at the end.

Graduate Students' Accounts of Duoethnography

Kari was an MA student of mine whom I invited to attend an ethnography workshop organized by Joe Norris and Rick Sawyer as part of a qualitative methodology conference in Banff in the fall of 2008. We attended with Sonia Aujla-Bhullar, another MA student whom she mentions below. She is currently a Vanier and SSHRC Bombardier Doctoral Scholar in the Faculty of Education at the University of British Columbia, and has published the duoethnography she co-wrote with Sonia.

Kari Grain: As for my experiences with duoethnography, the chapter Sonia and I wrote together (Aujla-Bhullar & Grain, 2012) was a way for me to understand that formative experiences as a teenager were directly related to how I worked with, in, and through social justice issues as an adult. Duoethnography showed me that discussing and unpacking these lived experiences with a colleague could actually serve as an activity that constructed new meaning and developed new data. I was raised to see "data" as numbers and "history" as a factual truth, so the duoethnography with Sonia was a way to acknowledge how my own history informs my current learning, and how face-to-face conversations are legitimate sources of data. It seems to bring the human back into the research process. I still struggle at times with the vulnerability of duoethnography, but I see vulnerability as essential to learning. How can we expect students and readers to embrace vulnerability if we are not willing to write and publish with some of that ourselves? It makes for a more honest and transparent research process.

Aubrey is a continuing doctoral student and new faculty member in the Werklund School of Education at the University of Calgary, and took a doctoral course on ethnographic research approaches from me in the winter of 2013:

Aubrey Hanson: As you know, I came to duoethnography in your ethnographic approaches to research course. I had not studied ethnography in any previous courses, and duoethnography actually helped ethnography make sense to me. That is, coming from a literary studies background and focusing on interpretive education research, duoethnography felt more familiar to me than ethnography generally. (Which is also likely because I was coming in with several interfering ideas of what ethnography might be; your course helped me grapple with those.) The kind of critical conversation that two people could have, pushing to understand each other's perspectives and making connections to experiences, readings, and social contexts, struck me as being both highly generative and personally responsible. Honestly, this kind of conversation is exactly the kind of deep conversation I would hope to have with colleagues on a good night out: not only to be engaged, but to really dig into something and find out how other people come to a topic. I left the class very excited to try a duoethnographic study of my own with a fellow graduate student. I believe that we can understand a topic better, and each other better as collaborators or critical interlocutors, if we make space for the kinds of explorations that duoethnography allows.

I also feel that learning about duoethnography has increased my appreciation of what interpretive education work brings to my own research. My research is on how Indigenous literatures connect to Indigenous communities, for instance, on how the narrative and pedagogical processes involved in taking up Indigenous literatures contribute to communities' resurgence and wellbeing. In many ways, this research is about strengthening the connections between academic work in Indigenous literary studies and Indigenous education. I did not initially intend to incorporate duoethnography into my research plan, but it came up unexpectedly for me when I was articulating the importance of understanding my own positioning. This emphasis on examining and explaining how one is situated in relation to a topic is prominent in Indigenous and interpretive approaches to research.

As I wrote this part of my dissertation proposal, I realized that duoethnography was one of the clearest examples from my graduate study in curriculum studies of how to examine one's own positioning critically, openly, and personally. Duoethnography enables scholars to do this work while building a relationship with each other; this process invokes interpersonal accountability, as each partner is interweaving critical perspectives with deeply personal experiences. I have much more digging to do in this area, but I know that duoethnography will influence how I understand critical reflexivity and positioning as I proceed with my doctoral research.

Kathleen is a former social worker whose doctoral program I supervised at the University of Calgary. She now holds a faculty position in Social Work at Memorial University in St. John's, Newfoundland and Labrador. She undertook a duoethnography with a colleague in social work around the topic of professional boundary issues with clients and it was eventually published in the first edited volume on the approach.

Kathleen Sitter: The strengths of duoethnography, including how we create new knowledge through discussion (and approaching a topic from differing social locations), became really apparent. The thoughtfulness of the dialogue and consciously keeping myself "open" to learning in this space was heightened during my own experience with writing a chapter with a colleague (Sitter & Hall, 2012). The power dynamic was also another key piece; it challenges the "researcher/researched" dichotomy, and in social justice research (and community-based action research, participatory, and collaborative approaches) where mitigating power is always a topic, I think this is an exemplar of how it is done on various levels.

The vulnerability is something that I found uncomfortable, especially since there is not an anonymous component; I often thought about this throughout the work. I particularly remember one point in our duoethnographic discussion where we began talking about religion. We were moving into an area that I found very personal, and I was cautious (and very purposeful) in how I framed my response. I have wondered if we had explored the option of anonymity in the work, might I have been more open to unpacking other ideas, or different areas about the topic?

This idea of being uncomfortable also reminded me of power, in particular having decision-making power in this context, which created a safe space. Part of the process Sean and I went through involved recording a conversation, transcribing, and going back and forth on building, reworking, and creating new paths in the conversation. I found this process empowering: I could change my mind on how I expressed my thoughts, and I had time to reflect on what it was I wanted to say, as well as my reaction and understanding to what Sean was saying. For me, it was a very thoughtful form of engagement, which I really appreciated, especially as I found it required that aspect of vulnerability.

Going through a duoethnographic "journey" and reflecting on these two ideas of vulnerability and power have impacted how I approach other forms of research, and my engagement with participants. I work in arts-based methods, where the work often finds itself in public spaces, such as exhibits and various digital platforms. When working with participants, the discussions about what it means to share visual stories are woven throughout the process, right from the beginning, so there are opportunities for people to change their mind about how or what they display or communicate in their visual stories.

David is an SSHRC Bombardier doctoral candidate in the Werklund School of Education, and is a Director of Student Experience in the B.Ed. program. He also took my course in ethnographic research approaches.

David Scott: Over the course of the 2013 winter term I was introduced to the methodological approach of duoethnography for the first time. As part of my final assignment I engaged in a duoethnographic dialogue with an Indigenous scholar, in which we explored the K-12 curricular directive in Alberta to take up social studies from Aboriginal perspectives (Alberta Education, 2010). During our conversations, we drew on our differing life histories and identity positions in order to explore the question of how a largely non-Aboriginal teaching community can meaningfully and ethically engage Aboriginal perspectives with their students.

Particularly for White Anglo-Canadian educators like me, in being asked to do this, we are in something of a Catch-22. We want to engage Aboriginal perspectives with our students in honorable and respectful ways; however, we have been educated within institutions of education that have sought to deny ways of knowing and being in the world unique to Indigenous oral traditions, communities, and peoples. As a result, social studies educators in Alberta are being asked to do something they do not necessarily know much about (Louie & Scott, 2016).

Below, I share three reasons why I think duoethnography is uniquely suited to grappling with difficult curricular questions like these, and can provide a viable alternative to what I see as the problematic nature of some prominent research methodologies in the field of education.

1. Duoethnography provides a way of doing research where participants are not treated as objects on which one's favored methodological approach is applied. Rather, it offers a more ethical participatory approach of doing research with, not on, other people;
2. Duoethnography does not seek to achieve the impossible task of bracketing out one's subjectivity in order to provide an account of "another's" point of view strictly from their point of view. Rather, this approach honors the voice of others on their own terms, in their own language and, moreover, foregrounds the subjectivity of the researcher. This can push both parties toward new transformative possibilities; and
3. Duoethnography does not arrive in the situation with the truth already known, as can be the case with some critical researchers who

> primarily seek to inform others of their victimization and oppression, rather than how we might work together to create a world that does justice to both of us.

Kimberley is an educator and doctoral candidate in the Werklund School of Education; she took my research course in ethnographic research approaches.

Kimberley Holmes: I was drowning in the depths of doctoral research courses, in phenomenology, hermeneutics, qualitative, quantitative, measurable, evidence-based data that needed to be analyzed, interpreted, and broken down into something that might one day resemble research to be used to actually make change in the world. Frankly, it was overwhelming, under-stimulating, and did not make a lot of sense to my storytelling heart. I am an English teacher, an aspiring poetic scholar, and a seeker of the human story and I was stuck among traditional methodologies that did not allow for creative voice and energy to emerge from an antiquated process of how things are done. I was attempting to be a doctoral student but the daunting rules and regulations surrounding the research process threated to keep me permanently submerged underneath the surface, struggling to find an open space to allow both me and my research to breathe. I needed a research methodology that allowed me to have control of my own learning, reflection on the process, and collaboration with others. I hoped to "enter into a conversation by revisiting my own school narratives, stories that when juxtaposed, may transform understanding and engender new insights" (Krammer & Mangiardi, 2012, p. 44). I had hoped for a creative, open space and was suffocating in the sea of rules, regulations, and protocol mandated by the past.

I needed to find some way back to storytelling and then seek a way to share that story with others, for our stories are not written in isolation but a collaborative chorus of many voices singing together. The melody would only emerge if my voice could be blended with others to create new patterns of understanding, new ways of being, and new ways of walking together in the world. I have always written a journal and documented the story of my own life. For me, writing is an intuitive process that allows a portal to my soul to be opened, purged, and then cleansed for renewal. It is a mindful, reflective process that allows me to come to a deeper understanding, so in some ways I have always been an autoethnographer—although I had no idea what that term meant when I started the doctoral journey. However, I had never considered the process of autoethnography as something that could be undertaken with another, although the concept made absolute sense to me. Indigenous societies have always known the value of sharing stories of our personal and collaborative cultures. Traditionally, this was how wisdom came into being, yet somehow this concept had eluded me in the digression of doctoral studies.

Hence, just when I was ready to go under the swirling sea of research methodologies the voice of the story called out to me again to be recognized as a catalyst for research data, and an opportunity to hear the human experience through the process of duoethnographic research. I was seeking something that was "soul searching, soul wrenching, and rewarding" (Norris et al., 2012, p. 11). I was tired of measuring and calculating, but on a quest for something deeper, more meaningful. My research question was looking at making change in pedagogical practice and I needed something to "inspire compassion and a sense of humanity" (p. 11). I needed something to call teachers to action, to allow them to recognize the faces of the learners and to bring us forward in this new educational paradigm. I needed somehow to access the "heart of wisdom" (Chambers, Leggo, Hasbe-Ludt, & Sinner, 2012) that would allow both my research participants and me to learn together what that might be.

I knew intuitively that this was how I needed to work and what I needed to do. My voice needed to merge with others around the sacred storytelling circle without a fixed design and predetermined destination. I needed to trust the process and let the story evolve. Duoethnography opened a space for this to happen. It allowed for "the dynamic interplay of two critically, questioning minds [to] transform, create, and expand each participant's understanding" (Krammer & Mangiardi, 2012, p. 43). It allowed me to return to my roots as a storyteller. Then it presented the opportunity to learn a new story, revisit the plot line, and find new meaning. I surfaced from the deep waters of doctoral research methodologies with a gasping breath of recognition. Another was sailing toward me in a raft gracefully gliding, without struggle or predetermined route. A smile crossed my face as I recognized the common vision. I swam strongly toward the other, and together through duoethnography we shared our stories and forged a new path to understanding.

Working with students has always been the most positive perk of my job as an educator, formerly as a high school teacher for 16 years, and for the past dozen or so as a university professor. Learning about the new methodology of duoethnography alongside a former high school student was both humbling and revelatory. Together, Rachel Evans and I recounted and analyzed our mutual experiences of forming the first gay–straight alliance high school program in the history of our province (Lund & Evans, 2006), in a piece that stands as the first refereed journal article using the approach. I was a new assistant professor at the time, and Rachel was an undergraduate student at another university. The methodology allowed us both to go beyond a retelling of the events as we remember them, to the critical examination of some of our own lived understandings of gender identity, sexuality, and activism. Our coming from different identity positions and discrepancy in age and life circumstances enhanced the quality of our conversation. Unpacking our biographical baggage allowed a deeper way of uncovering the topic, and opened a vulnerability that is arguably unusual in academic work. Rachel and I used email correspondence to open up and organize our dialogue, and our conversation continued intermittently over a few months. Our reciprocal research project proved to be a highly personal and intellectually engaging experience at the same time. We have since co-presented our findings at conferences, and recently revisited our earlier collaboration to write duoethnographically about our understandings of ethics in teacher–student advisory relationships (see Evans & Lund, 2013). I have also invited Rachel on occasion to speak to my diversity-themed courses in a B.Ed. program and we continue to keep in touch. Our ongoing collaborations and friendship serve for me as an illustration of the many benefits and spinoff perks of a duoethnographic research approach.

In a similar manner, I have developed a very positive and productive research relationship with Dr. Maryam Nabavi, whose community work in youth activism brought our research together. She was coordinating a highly successful local student social justice group called "Youth ROAR (Reach Out Against Racism)" and I was on the advisory committee to the group for about six years. After she had completed a master's degree in the area, we undertook a few collaborative projects together interviewing students and teachers who had undertaken social justice activism in schools and communities. Beginning a duoethnography on approaching this work from two very different identity positions allowed us to arrive at some important insights into how our own positionality has affected all aspects of our antiracist work. As Maryam remarked, "it is interesting how we can access these parts of our memory and with the lens through which we live our lives now see those conversations—positive or negative—about race as subsequently forming our respective racial identities" (Lund & Nabavi, 2008, p. 29). Our candid reflections were rooted in our life experiences, and brought us to understandings that we could not have reached on our own. When we had a chance to conduct a further duoethnographic conversation for the first edited collection on the methodology, we welcomed the chance to delve even further into our own life histories to trace our personal curricula of difference growing up in Canada. In our case, it was a dialogue on identity and belonging between a woman of color who arrived as a refugee and a member of the dominant White European identity with a childhood rife with unflattering experiences with difference. Our conversation went places that opened up new ways of seeing ourselves today; at one point I wrote, "our complex notions of citizenship and belonging have many layers, but often these are unspoken and unexamined; even this conversation feels strained and discomforting" (Nabavi & Lund, 2012, p. 182). We decided to leave such moments in the account, as a way of noting these points of self-consciousness, discomfort, and, in some cases, regret and shame. These personal examples of racism from both the perpetrator and receiver angle helped us to ground our broader discussions and analyses of systemic and institutionalized forms of oppression, situating our lived experiences within a larger sociopolitical context.

Discussion

Each of the invited co-authors to this chapter has shared personal perspectives of engaging with duoethnography in some manner as part of a graduate studies program. Attending to their perspectives can help us learn how this dialogic approach to research has opened up new ways for them of understanding their research and themselves. Perhaps the most salient and frequently echoed theme is around building interpersonal accountability through collaboration. In using duoethnographic dialogue, students were able to find ways to build empathy with others who had diverse life experiences and views. Their efforts toward discussing a common topic or theme and making connections afforded them a chance to critically examine their own history and their own positions, all within the framework of their own identity. The approach requires an articulation of one's belief systems at some point, and highlights subjectivity. Therefore, rather than having to "bracket out" their individual differences, duoethnography encourages participants to "bracket in." As Sawyer and Norris (2013) explain, "central to bracketing in is that subjective identity and personal epistemology are foregrounded as a focus of analysis" (p. 15). Presuppositions and biases are not ignored or set aside but exposed and articulated as part of the site of collaborative dialogic inquiry.

Research is the creation of new knowledge and this approach fosters the co-creation of new understandings and insights that would have been impossible to gain without the other participant. Both are co-researchers, creating new knowledge through dialogue. As Willis and Siltanen (2009) discovered in their own collaborative research, "our multiple and constantly shifting 'voices' provided an essential interpretive resource, enabling us to develop a thick and common understanding of the subject/object of research" (p. 109). This shared meaning-making involves both collective and individual reflection, and a necessary focus on one's own biography, identity, and positionality from the outset. Just as with any form of ethnography that employs a critical sensibility, with social justice and equity at its heart, duoethnography requires some often challenging self-reflection throughout. In describing ethnography more generally, Madden (2010) reflects that,

> in my case, a critical appreciation of positionality is a tool with which to check my ethnographic baggage for resumption and prejudice; to remind myself I bring just one perspective to ethnography and that perspective is informed by my own upbringing, education and history. (p. 22)

With the dual nature of duoethnographies, it is essential that both parties understand this from the start and build this difficult work into the process.

Part of the nature of this kind of highly personal engagement with another person in a research relationship are the additional elements of the researchers' vulnerabilities and risks, issues not as strongly associated with other forms of academic research. However, as Freire (1998) reminds us, "coherent democratic authority recognizes the ethical basis of our presence in the world and necessarily recognizes that it is not possible to live ethically without freedom and that there is no such thing as freedom without risk" (p. 87). A high degree of trust is required between participants, and both are mutually responsible for the creation of the collaboratively composed duoethnography. This reciprocally driven research has the effect of putting both participants on a much more level playing field. Power and positionality are not erased or downplayed, but, rather, are foregrounded and addressed directly throughout the engagement. The accounts above confirm my own experiences of an approach that seems more effective at mitigating power and privilege differentials in an open and deliberate manner. Inevitably, this orientation allows for a much more consciously ethical treatment of both research participants than a typical object/subject orientation in top-down academic research models.

Perhaps even more than most qualitative research approaches, duoethnography privileges and elucidates individual subjectivity, requiring a "bracketing in" as mentioned above versus the more common efforts to "bracket out" idiosyncratic viewpoints, cultural influences, historical situation, and other dimensions of the social context in which all research takes place. The rich complexities of our lived worlds are not stripped of nuance or subjectivity, but elucidated and held up more transparently to analysis along with our personal narratives within those settings and identity positions. In a related way, duoethnography also requires and values storytelling, and encourages listening intently to the human experience around particular topics. In this manner, the collaboration of two or more people toward this end offers rich interpretive possibilities. As Steeves et al. (2009) argue, "if dialogue enables the opening up and restorying of the selves involved in research and of interpretive possibilities, then collective approaches to research ought to be valued highly" (p. 122). Avoiding a priori truth claims and remaining open to new insights into human experiences and new understandings of shared topics allow duoethographers a rich opportunity to co-create knowledge within a trusting dialogic relationship.

Conclusion

Through the accounts and discussion in this chapter, I situate this promotion of duoethnography and other forms of dialogic research and inquiry as an approach that has the courage to create a counterstory that resists neoliberalism. Steeves et al. (2009) describe their collaborative narrative work in just such a manner:

> We see this as a way of composing a counterstory of what matters in research, a counterstory threaded not around funding, publications and ownership, but around the possibility of creating educative spaces … to imagine and live out what seems impossible on our own, but becomes possible within these relational spaces. (pp. 58–59)

Drawing on their own experiences and perspectives, each of the graduate student contributors above used specific instances and illustrations to share what worked for them in this dialogic approach. Also included was the recognition of some of the challenges associated with the approach. I trust that their articulate descriptions of the joys, vulnerabilities, and promises of duoethnography may stand as a strong incentive for others to include this research approach in their graduate teaching, to make use of this and other robust and ethical research models in creating a more humane and authentically collaborative climate within the academy.

With each university course I teach, and with each of the students who takes up a duoethnographic approach in his or her own way, I am encouraged by the wide range of possibilities for its application in social science research. As attested to above, and elucidated in each of these accounts, there are many forms it can take and the myriad ways that its dialogic nature can draw people together to create more meaningful engagements across difference. Echoed in each account is a recognition of how this approach stands in opposition to dehumanizing discourses and practices that are all too common in our increasingly market-driven and neoliberal institutions.

In many ways, I wish for the duoethnographic approach to represent a signal of hope for the new McUniversity, as coined by Ritzer (2014). He concluded:

> Hope, if there is any, lies in the objects of education: the students. They can be seen as engaging in a fatal strategy by seeming to accept all the changes the postmodern educational system throws at them. While we usually think power resides with the educational systems, it could be argued that it is the mass of students who have the power. (p. 195)

One way that students and other scholars can exercise their power to resist the neoliberal market forces of the academy is to engage in deliberate acts of humanizing dialogue to reclaim this space. Borrowing the words of Hedges (2010), I believe researchers can adopt duoethnography and other dialogic research approaches "to continue to fight the mechanisms of that dominant culture, if for no other reason than to preserve, through small, even tiny acts, our common humanity" (p. 217).

References

Alberta Education. (2010). *Program of studies for Social Studies 30-1*. Edmonton, AB: Alberta Education, Government of Alberta.

Aujla-Bhullar, S., & Grain, K. M. (2012). Mirror imaging diversity experiences: A juxtaposition of identities in cross-cultural initiatives. In J. Norris, R. D. Sawyer, & D. E. Lund (Eds.), *Duoethnography: Dialogic methods for social, health, and educational research* (pp. 199–222). Walnut Creek, CA: Left Coast Press.

Ayers, W. (2001). *To teach: The journey of a teacher* (2nd ed.). New York, NY: Teachers College Press.

Chambers, C. M., Hasbe-Ludt, E., Leggo, C., & Sinner, A. (Eds.). (2012). *A heart of wisdom.* New York, NY: Peter Lang.

Evans, R. E., & Lund, D. E. (2013). Forging ethical adult-youth relationships within emancipatory activism. *International Journal of Child, Youth and Family Studies, 3*(1), 433–443. Retrieved from http://journals.uvic.ca/index.php/ijcyfs/issue/view/707

Freire, P. (1998). *Pedagogy of freedom: Ethics, democracy, and civic courage.* Lanham, MD: Rowman & Littlefield.

Giroux, H. A. (2010). Bare pedagogy and the scourge of neoliberalism: Rethinking higher education as a democratic public sphere. *The Educational Forum, 74*(3), 184–196.

Giroux, H. A. (2011). *Zombie politics and culture in the age of casino capitalism.* New York, NY: Peter Lang.

Glaser, E. (2015, May 21). Bureaucracy: Why won't scholars break their paper chains? *Times Higher Education.* 10 para. Retrieved from http://www.timeshighereducation.co.uk/features/bureaucracy-why-wont-scholars-break--their-paper-chains/2/2020256.article

Hedges, C. (2010). *Death of the liberal class.* New York, NY: Nation Books.

Jubas, K., & Seidel, J. (2014). Knitting as metaphor for work: An institutional autoethnography to surface tensions of visibility and invisibility in the neoliberal academy. *Journal of Contemporary Ethnography,* 1–25. doi:10.1177/0891241614550200.

Krammer, D., & Mangiardi, R. (2012). The hidden curriculum of schooling: A duoethnographic exploration of what schools teach us about schooling. In J. Norris, R. D. Sawyer, & D. E. Lund (Eds.), *Duoethnography: Dialogic methods for social, health, and educational research* (pp. 41–70). Walnut Creek, CA: Left Coast Press.

Louie, D. W., & Scott, D. (2016). Examining differing notions of a "real" education within Aboriginal communities. *Critical Education, 7*(3), 1–18.

Lund, D. E., & Evans, R. E. (2006). Opening a can of worms: A duo-ethnographic dialogue on gender, orientation and activism. *Taboo: The Journal of Culture and Education, 10*(2), 55–67.

Lund, D. E., & Nabavi, M. (2008). A duo-ethnographic conversation on social justice activism: Exploring issues of identity, racism, and activism with young people. *Multicultural Education, 15*(4), 27–32.

Madden, R. (2010). *Being ethnographic: A guide to the theory and practice of ethnography.* Thousand Oaks, CA: Sage.

Nabavi, M., & Lund, D. E. (2012). The tensions and contradictions of living in a multicultural nation in an era of bounded identities. In J. Norris, R. D. Sawyer, & D. E. Lund (Eds.), *Duoethnography: Dialogic methods for social, health, and educational research* (pp. 177–197). Walnut Creek, CA: Left Coast Press.

Norris, J. (2008). Duoethnography. In L. M. Given (Ed.), *The SAGE encyclopedia of qualitative research methods* (pp. 233–236). Thousand Oaks, CA: Sage.

Norris, J., & Sawyer, R. (2004). Null and hidden curricula of sexual orientation: A dialogue on the curreres of the absent presence and the present absence. In L. Coia, M. Birch, N. J. Brooks, E. Heilman, S. Mayer, A. Mountain, & P. Pritchard (Eds.), *Democratic responses in an era of standardization* (pp. 139–159). Troy, NY: Educator's International Press.

Norris, J., & Sawyer, R. (2005, February). *The curriculum of sexual orientation as lived by a gay straight male and a straight gay male.* Paper presented at "Provoking Curriculum: To Promote a New Era of Canadian Curriculum Questioning," a symposium of the Canadian Association of Curriculum Studies, Victoria, BC.

Norris, J., Sawyer, R. D., & Lund, D. E. (Eds.). (2012). *Duoethnography: Dialogic methods for social, health, and educational research.* Walnut Creek, CA: Left Coast Press.

Panayotidis, E. L., Lund, D. E., Towers, J., & Smits, H. (2016). Worldlessness and wordlessness: How might we talk about teacher education in a fractured world? *Critical Education, 7*(7), 1–23.

Ritzer, G. (2014). McUniversity in the postmodern consumer society. *Quality in Higher Education, 2*(3), 185–199. doi:10.1080/1353832960020302.

Sameshima, P. (2013). Understanding qualitative research and duoethnography: Promoting personal and societal change within dialogic self-study. *Journal of the Canadian Association for Curriculum Studies, 11*(1), 1–20. Retrieved from http://www.jcacs.com/#!v111aduoethnography-understanding-q/c17c

Sawyer, R. D., & Norris, J. (2013). *Understanding qualitative research: Duoethnography.* Oxford University Press: New York, NY.

Sitter, K. C., & Hall, S. (2012). Professional boundaries: Creating space and getting to the margins. In J. Norris, R. D. Sawyer, & D. E. Lund (Eds.), *Duoethnography: Dialogic methods for social, health, and educational research* (pp. 243–260). Walnut Creek, CA: Left Coast Press.

Steeves, P., Pearce, M., Orr, A. M., Murphy, S. M., Huber, M., Huber, J., & Clandinin, D. J. (2009). What we know first: Interrupting the institutional narrative of individualism. In W. S. Gershon (Ed.), *The collaborative turn: Working together in qualitative research* (pp. 55–69). Rotterdam, The Netherlands: Sense.

Willis, A., & Siltanen, J. (2009). Restorying work inside and outside the academy: Practices of reflexive team research. In W. S. Gershon (Ed.), *The collaborative turn: Working together in qualitative research* (pp. 105–125). Rotterdam, The Netherlands: Sense.

CHAPTER 7

Community, Identity, and Graduate Education: Using Duoethnography as a Mechanism for Forging Connections in Academia

Claudia Diaz and Kari Grain

Introduction

Research in graduate studies indicates that students face struggles with isolation, loneliness, and a lacking sense of community (Cotterall, 2013; McAlpine & Norton, 2006) as education becomes increasingly pragmatic, focusing on measurable outcomes such as publication records, grades, and completion rates that strengthen the likelihood of career success (Pinar, 2011). In order to meet increasingly globalized and technologized educational goals that pivot on capitalist demands for productivity, university students and educators in the West are spending less time in the type of face-to-face interactions that can serve as catalysts for reflexivity, vulnerability, and community. When this issue is added to that of a highly competitive job market for professorships, and a decline in tenure-track positions, it becomes clear that graduate students and their educators face

C. Diaz (✉) • K. Grain
University of British Columbia, Vancouver, BC, Canada

J. Norris, *Theorizing Curriculum Studies, Teacher Education, and Research through Duoethnographic Pedagogy*,
DOI 10.1057/978-1-137-51745-6_7

formidable challenges in terms of academic success on the one hand and well-being on the other.

Our own experience as doctoral students has illustrated how an enhanced sense of community, access to opportunities for face-to-face interaction, and peer support strengthen our capacity to learn course content and approach our work as more confident learners and scholars. Additional research also shows that collaborative peer support enables and deepens the graduate learning process (Devenish et al., 2009). We suggest that graduate student struggles are symptoms of a system that is in crisis over its misplaced emphasis on control and regulation, thereby positioning competition (as opposed to community) as its key value. Therefore, in this chapter, we contend that the use of duoethnography as a component of graduate education may, as a primary benefit, contest this misplaced emphasis on competition, regulation, and standardization; and as a secondary benefit, duoethnography, in our experience, serves to alleviate stressors to graduate students' well-being through its focus on collaboration and reflexivity. In this way, duoethnography may serve students as a pedagogy and methodology for political contestation.

While duoethnography has become a burgeoning methodology in its own right, there is less literature outlining its curricular and pedagogical possibilities, and our aim is to develop these aspects using concepts already embedded in duoethnography. This chapter builds on Joe Norris' use of duoethnography to "assist graduate students in examining their life histories to determine how their curriculum of a concept …influences their beliefs and behaviours" (Norris, 2008, p. 233). In other words, duoethnography is identified as a way that learners might examine their understanding of a particular idea in relation to their lived narratives. In tandem with this idea, we use the work of William Pinar to delve into an expansion of how we conceive of and think about curriculum; in particular, we draw on Pinar's notion of *currere*, understood as lived experience that comprises an informal, everyday curriculum (Pinar, 1975). In the graduate school context, the value of conversation and reflexivity can be overlooked in favor of standardized institutional or curricular learning expectations, or what Pinar (2011) called a "curriculum of functionality" (p. 2), which can sometimes lead to a lack of scholarly community and connection. This problem foregrounds the potential of duoethnography not only as a research methodology but also as a pedagogy for collaborative self-examination. As doctoral students in the University of British Columbia's Faculty of Education, we have encountered continuous tensions around our identities—as influenced by different histories and privileges—and our roles as researchers, learners, and educators. We sought a way to weave together these different dimensions and develop a scholarly identity, a process that Thomson and Walker (2010) propose is deeply embedded in the success of doctoral students.

To work through this dilemma, we drew on duoethnography's tenets to structure a three-month project in which we met weekly for two hours, using a duoethnographic conversation each week to address the question: How can we navigate these tensions by collaboratively examining and challenging our histories and assumptions? In our first meeting, after having decided to use duoethnography as our mode of inquiry, we discussed some key structural elements that we agreed to maintain throughout the project to ensure consistency, while also remaining flexible. Each week consisted of a recursive dialogue not only between ourselves, but also between our duoethnographic conversation (face-to-face) and our reflections (written privately) that we shared with one another after—and in response to—our most recent conversation. After each meeting we chose a question to inspire our written reflection. The questions were targeted to each of us individually based on the unique issues we faced. For example, questions included how have your experiences as a volunteer in Ghana shaped your understanding of privilege? How are your childhood experiences of attending a public school in Chile intertwined with your current tension with privilege? As such, every week's dialogue built upon the previous week's understanding and revealed an evolving focus for our conversations.

This project culminated in one recorded duoethnography session, wherein we reflected upon our three-month process, using our conversations and written reflection documents as "cultural artifacts" (Chang, 2008). We position them as cultural artifacts because they reflect our personal experiences in a particular socio-cultural context, thereby providing material to examine a wider societal structure. Throughout this chapter, we offer an illustration of our doctoral program context and the avenue by which we came to use duoethnography to address the locus of our inquiry. We then describe the theoretical framework that informs our research and analysis, borrowing heavily from ideas in curriculum reconceptualization and social justice work. Throughout this chapter, we aim to envision how duoethnography can be a methodology that contests a doctoral program's curriculum of functionality—that is, a curriculum driven by standardization and examination—and facilitates the collaborative exploration of Pinar's (1975) notion of *currere*. For our analysis and interpretation we critically examine, first, the set of written reflections and notes from our three-month project. Afterward, we examine a recorded duoethnographic session containing dialogue on how we used duoethnography in our graduate program as a methodology and pedagogy for working through and moving beyond ethical and identity-related tensions. These two sources had distinct purposes: the purpose of our weekly sessions was to explore our conflicting relationship between privilege and scholarly identity; our recorded duoethnography, however, was meant to reflect upon how duoethnography helped us to understand how this methodology was helpful for us in our process of learning, and what it did for us practically, as an embodiment of community building. We organize our analysis and interpretation into three themes: (1) Embarking on our duoethnography: Binaries and privilege; (2) Sites of research: Ourselves; and (3) Transtemporal Transformation. Our initial inclination when we embarked upon this journey was to eliminate our uncomfortable tension in our learning process; however, as we employed this methodology, we came to understand tension as essential to our transformative learning. We conclude this chapter with some closing thoughts on the use of duoethnography in the construction of community, the development of identity, and the problematization of the "functional curriculum" of traditional graduate programs. Our duoethnography project resulted in a transformation of our previously learned assumptions around privilege, social justice, and constructed binaries. Through duoethnography, rather than solving our tensions, we re-imagined how complex and contradictory identities can be valuable in the educational process. Finally, we examine how duoethnography was useful in our case, not only pedagogically and curricularly, but also in a way that contributed to our emotional well-being.

Our Doctoral Program Context

We did not begin this journey of learning with duoethnography in mind. Instead, we began with a problem, an unmistakable *tension*: As first year doctoral students in educational studies, we were both grappling with a dissonance between our individual histories (of relative privilege) and the academic futures that our graduate program curriculum was promoting. We were each stuck in a sort of liminal, temporal space between who we once were and who we were expected to become: A researcher, an expert, an educator—a "knower" of social justice approaches in education. In the brief moments when our classroom learning would examine this tension, we both experienced a palpable sense of discomfort and ambiguity, which we quickly "bracketed" (see Gearing, 2008; Norris, 2008) in order to attend to course readings and outcomes. Gearing (2008) describes bracketing as a "rigorous process that suspends internal and external suppositions, thereby allowing the focusing in on a specific phenomenon in order to understand or see it as it is" (p. 64). In contestation of this concept, and in line with Norris (2008), duoethnography actually encourages researchers to "bracket in" their own suppositions, experiences, and affective responses to various ideas and concepts. Thus, later on in our duoethnographic process, we learned that "bracketing ourselves in" allows us to make our life experiences a site for reflection and learning. This discomfort may be partially attributed to the format and structure of our class environment, but also arises because there are some points of tension that are difficult to explore in an open class format, as opposed to in one-on-one interactions. In some ways, we could not learn or absorb our content knowledge until we had worked through some deeper questions around how we had built our identity in relation to social justice, and what we desired in terms of community and our place in that web of interconnections. Before we could learn the functional content of our classroom instruction, we recognized the necessity of initiating vulnerable, critical self-examination around our positionalities, our assumptions, and our epistemologies. This process occurs ideally alongside the curriculum in simultaneity, as opposed to before or after, in a linear or teleological conception of learning.

In this chapter the pronoun "we" refers to Claudia Díaz and Kari Grain, both doctoral students in the Department of Educational Studies of the University of British Columbia. Claudia is also a Chilean international doctoral student and a mother, and a former social practitioner and child advocate whose interest in children's experiences in education in contexts marked by poverty, marginalization, and exclusion came from her years as Psychology's student in Chile. After graduating as a Community Psychologist, she worked for ten years as a manager in socio-educational and poverty reduction programs and as an activist in grassroots organizations. This experience was crucial in her interest in children's experiences and lives embedded in socio-political contexts that trouble the promise of social mobility and educational equity through education in marginalized neighborhoods. Aware of her current privileged position as a researcher, she engaged in this duoethnographic process to unpack the dilemmas in researching marginalized communities.

Kari, like Claudia, is a doctoral student in Vancouver, Canada, and has spent more than a decade working with issues of poverty, marginalization, and social justice. As an undergraduate and master's student, she participated in a number of transformative experiential education programs that drew attention to the Holocaust, the Rwandan genocide, and other global injustices; these programs led her to non-profit work in educational contexts, where she developed and facilitated anti-racism workshops, interfaith experiences, and education programs for immigrant and refugee youth. Her master's research examined the narratives of volunteer teachers in Rwanda and foregrounded salient issues of race, colonialism, and problematic helping narratives in the realm of international engagement practices. The at times intensely emotional nature of experiential learning programs led her to her current doctoral research around the role of emotions in international service learning and other forms of global engagement. Using her identity as a Canadian-born, white woman to personally observe and interact with tensions around privilege, race, and inequality, she aims to simultaneously critique Western notions of "helping" while also appreciating the value of cooperation and collaboration.

Pinar (2011) proposes that a "curriculum of functionality" and its consequential focus on learning outcomes has the potential to supersede the process and nuances that comprise learning in specific locations, moments, and cultures (p. 2). Throughout our classes and, indeed, throughout most research methodologies to which we had been exposed, we bracketed out our individual narratives and meaning-making in favor of pre-existing discourse and taken-for-granted truths. To illustrate this, we shared a sense of discomfort in a classroom discussion focused on case study, wherein we were both distracted by the implications of being privileged researchers in a marginalized community. As learners, as researchers, and as people invested in the work of social justice, we were hungry for a way to "bracket in" (Norris, 2008) the complexities of our current and historical being, while also attending to important epistemological and theoretical questions inherent in a doctoral education. Most of all, we struggled with the evolving significance of our individual privilege, and how the changing face of that privilege might play out ethically in our work. We were both concerned with how we might go about being anti-oppressive researchers when we come from places of relative privilege. Using Karen Potts and Leslie Brown's (2005) strategies for anti-oppressive research, we acknowledge that we have the potential at all times to be both the oppressor and the oppressed, and this is a continuous, fluid divergence at all times, but especially in our roles as researchers with underprivileged communities.

This, however, is not to say that our tensions or identities were similar in nature. The crux of Claudia's struggle related to her childhood conceptions of poverty and privilege, as illustrated by her experiences in Chile's hierarchical public and private school systems. Her tension was made more complex by her present-day privilege as a Chilean doctoral student in a prestigious Canadian university. Kari's tension, on the other hand, was oriented in a dissonance between her instinctive inclination to nurture her idealism, and an equally pronounced desire to problematize that idealism in relation to her identity as a middle-class, white Canadian woman. Her disorientation lay in a constant swing between what felt like two polarities of idealism and cynicism, leaving her unsure which seemingly contradictory voice to use in her work.

Having learned a great deal through a former duoethnography chapter that Kari and her colleague Sonia Aujla-Bhullar had published in *Duoethnography: Dialogic Methods for Social, Health, and Educational Research* (Aujla-Bhullar & Grain, 2010), Kari suggested during our first meeting that this methodology may actually serve us as a pedagogical tool in understanding our own lived curriculum as a jumping-off point for our doctoral journeys. Referring to Sawyer and Norris' (2013) publication, *Duoethnography: Understanding Qualitative Research*, we identified that, indeed, our line of inquiry might be effectively examined via duoethnography's "living tenets." In particular, our goal of navigating and reflecting upon some identified tensions could be well served by duoethnography tenets related to bracketing in our voices, (re)storying ourselves and our conceptions of the other, recognizing identities as fluid and shifting, and trusting one another in dialogues around power differentials (Sawyer & Norris, 2013). In these ways and others, duoethnography appeared to provide a means within academia to undergo this necessary reflection to "dialogically critique and question the meanings (we) give to social issues and epistemological constructs" (Sawyer & Norris, 2013, p. 2). Through the use of duoethnography, we contest and recast the curriculum of functionality, acknowledging and celebrating the messy nuances and historical foundations of our particular lived realities. We thus agreed to meet on a weekly basis over three months, to engage in duoethnographic discussions wherein we began to "read the self as text" (Sawyer & Norris, 2013, p. 15), thereby exploring duoethnography in its capacity as a pedagogy.

Curriculum of Functionality

This chapter, like duoethnography itself, is heavily influenced by the work of William Pinar, who, in his reconceptualization of curriculum, contended that school curriculum must attend to socio-cultural intricacies in order to be useful in the quest for societal improvement (1978). In place of procedural, prescriptive curriculum development with universalized content and approaches, Pinar illustrated a vision of curriculum development that is lived through unique subjectivities, ever-transforming ways of being in the world, and often painful, messy, and contested histories. Following that, the possibility of curriculum for Pinar neither ceases in its meaning at the temporal edges of class time, nor is it a force that lives only inside the four-walled classroom, catering to a set of prescribed outcomes. Instead, curriculum development might serve to honor the unique ways in which learners' histories become their voices, their bodies, their means for understanding. Curriculum for Pinar then becomes *currere*: a thing of flexibility and specificity—a possibility that lives in and with the learner at every moment (1975).

Conceived this way, we felt that the "curriculum of functionality" that undergirded our graduate program was premised on outcomes related to success within a traditional institutional structure: skills for peer-reviewed publication success and an understanding of seminal theoretical scholars (and a subsequent, if unintentional marginalization or exclusion of "other" voices in our field). We are aware of the challenges of contesting and escaping these demands since we are part of a current academic system in which we aspire to have voices and be heard for our perspectives that advocate for change. Nonetheless, we propose that the academic endeavor can be carried out with expanded, more diverse purposes than strictly functionality. For example, what kind of knowledge do we need to develop in order to achieve social transformation? What is our responsibility to others in this particular place and historical moment? Thus, we simultaneously felt engaged with our learning, while also acknowledging a hunger for a deeper connection between that content and our personal struggles around community and an evolving sense of identity. As such, we were inclined to *extend* and *stretch* this curriculum so that it could somehow be integrated into our lived realities. There is, in this moment, a dissonance between the curriculum that is meant to be functional and the understanding that it can only serve us functionally if it *fits* us as individuals—individuals with unique histories, injuries, and locations that continue to shape us. Extending that, we suggest here that duoethnography became a means for us as graduate students to face the curriculum, try it on, and explore how its dimensions could become flexible according to our specificities or what Pinar would call our *currere*.

Our Duoethnography Process

This section contains our duoethnographic process through a polyvocal text (Norris, Sawyer, & Lund, 2012) that bring our identities and stories in a continuous dialogue. However, our experiences and narratives are not presented as traditional duoethnographies, which tend to be written in script format, dialectically moving from one participant to the other. We present our duoethnography as a process in which we identify three main moments: (1) embarking on our duoethnography through binaries and privilege, (2) engaging ourselves as sites of research; and (3) undergoing a transtemporal transformation. This organization seeks to illustrate why our duoethnography is distinguished from a typical conversation in which the identities who are speaking are not necessary at stake. As with conversation in general, the start and end points are artificial since conversations go beyond the limits of time and contain many starting and ending points simultaneously and continuously. Through this particular form of organizing our polyvocal texts, our intention is to illustrate how duoethnography can serve graduate students and their educators as pedagogy and curriculum.

1. Embarking on Our Duoethnography: Binaries and Privilege

Following Norris and Sawyer's (2004) first duoethnography, which examined sexual orientation in a heteronormatively framed world, we developed our duoethnography to examine the role of privilege in the development of our own scholarly identity. Reading and discussing in class a wide range of literature on social justice, we felt an unintelligible tension that we attempted to unpack/disentangle in our class conversations but simultaneously we did not find it appropriate to expose our inner conflicts as topics for academic conversations in the classroom. We believed that our struggles, rife with discomfort, existed in a different realm than academic knowledge, so we initially sought a more intimate, private means to engage with our questions. In this context, duoethnography offered us a means by which we could draw on personal lived experiences as sources for research and analysis through collaborative engagement with academic texts and ideas.

Although we shared a common conflict between our own privileges and our future scholarly identities, we experienced that tension differently. Kari found herself perpetually problematizing her identity as a middle-class, white woman working with social justice issues, whereas Claudia felt that being a privileged graduate student in a Western university (as opposed to a Chilean or Latin American university) was somehow problematic. We each encountered nuanced combinations of guilt, hypocrisy, and criticality, which, at the time, we felt must be resolved; we had not yet considered the possibility of living in and with that discomfort, and what it might mean to do so. One source of discomfort lay in our privileged position in a global context, highlighting issues such as north–south poverty differentials, sustainability, and colonialism. On the other hand, we face daily social justice issues in our local context, as our university is located on unceded Musqueam land, thereby raising questions of neo-colonialism and unsettling settler relations; further, we are daily witnesses to and participants in a climate of inequity for limited graduate student funding opportunities. And we need not venture far from campus to witness salient issues of poverty, marginalization, and drug abuse in broader Vancouver communities. In light of the complexities and inequalities locally and globally, our project helped us to realize that perhaps the crux of the problem lay in our assumption that such discomfort can be "solved" or "overcome." Kari's conflict was further illustrated by her comments about her own privilege. Referring to her mother's stories of immigration from Norway, she said:

> I have this conflicting history surrounding my mother's immigration stories, knowing that it was indeed difficult for her, but also knowing that her visual appearance helped her to feel a part of the normative culture, perhaps without her even realizing it. But one thing I know for sure is that I did not earn many of the privileges I carry around every day as a white person. Have I worked hard? Yes of course. Did my grandparents work hard to establish a new life in Canada? Of course. But millions of people work hard, and very few of them get opportunities to travel the world, live in a safe neighbourhood, and in my case, work toward a PhD. So as a researcher,

> I am experiencing this tremendous conflict between how I (the idealist) feel about humans and migration and difference (diversity is beautiful and joyful, and we need to work together to learn from one another and love one another—this perspective feels unsettlingly similar to a neoliberal one ...) and how I (the critic) think about the same things (colonialism and white privilege created this society that privileges me and does not privilege others, and I am complicit in inequality regardless of what I do).

We came to problematize why and how privilege contradicts the development of an integral scholarly identity. We found that the core of our conflict was related to binary conceptions. Kari's tensions between her idealistic self on the one hand and her critical self on the other illustrated how entrenched the construction of assumed binaries can be in our perceptions. Kari continued,

> I have struggled all year with what I thought was a dissonance of two different voices and different selves. I am an idealist in my heart—and have lived a life that allows me that luxury. Yet, I am a critic in my mind. I have spent the past eight months as a divided human who doesn't know or understand which voice to use as I embark on the journey of academia, and this division has felt frustrating and disorienting. Finding my voice is still difficult.

As we unpacked our narratives of privilege, we began to realize that our conflicts were merely gateways for other conversations about privilege: How/when did we learn who is privileged and who is not? What were our own experiences with privilege growing up? Do privilege and social justice contradict one another, and, if so, in what ways? How do our histories in this realm interact with our identities as scholars in social justice? How might our gender play a role in our research, struggles, and scholar identity? As we developed these lines of inquiry, we came to notice how we ourselves could be valuable as sites of research.

2. Sites of Research: Ourselves

As we mentioned earlier, we did not initially intend to carry out a duoethnography for our inquiry. We hoped simply to learn more about the source of our discomfort in our doctoral program. However, duoethnography's flexible structure allowed us to use it not in prescriptive but in emergent ways (Sawyer & Norris, 2013). In addition to principles of social justice, duoethnography has drawn on autoethnography and narrative to challenge dominant discourses, so it seemed to be a natural tool that we could use for our own learning goals. Embedded in these stories we found valuable material to examine dominant discourses and power relationships we have taken for granted so far.

Discussing her childhood experiences of social class, Claudia recalled,

> In contrast with my grandparents' stories of poverty, la Minita, who raised my Grandma, came from a sophisticated and affluent family. All the fancy stuff that surrounded my childhood home was hers. She used to hold parties with other active socialite families and her presence was the daily reminder of the differences between social classes and somehow the social class hierarchy. The predominance of social class as a social category was not only a distinctive aspect of my own family, but this was also replicated in many of the social spaces that I used to be when I was a child: the neighborhood, the school, the public square, and the church.

Engaging with an examination of her social, cultural, and geographic childhood contexts, Claudia identified how her continuous transitions between home and school and private and public school informed her understanding of social class hierarchy. She continued,

> To be or not to be poor was an identity marker from an early age for me. I understood and felt the disadvantages of being poor as somebody who lacked in dignity. I attended both private and public schools and I lived in a suburb middle class neighborhood 15 minutes away from the neighbors where my public-school classmates lived, so I transited every day in between two social class worlds in which housing, studying, working, having fun were different in form according to social class. I was quite sensitive to differences between all these practices and I was afraid to be identified as poor.

3. Transtemporal Transformation

The narration of our memories was not only an exercise of examination but also one of transformation. As Ng-A-Fock and Milne (2014) wrote: "life writing as shadow texts, as currere, enables us to revisit the past as a practice of unsettling the present" (p. 2). During narration, the present helped us to reconceptualize the past as well as the past helped us to reconceptualize the present. As we shared our childhood stories we had an opportunity to foreground our unique ways of understanding experience. However, this learning was not fixed. Rather, it was subject to change through a critical collaboration with each other, wherein probing and further questioning was necessary for transformation. Although our initial sense of transformation was rather to change our discomfort by understanding the substance of it, we came to realize that the duoethnographic process helped us to understand transformation in a temporal continuum in which both past and present were transformed by critical questions. As Sawyer and Norris (2013) articulate, the goal of duoethnography is for researchers to "seek not commonalities but differences as they collaboratively develop a transformative text" (p. 88). The collaboration between two researchers distinguishes duoethnography from autoethnography. As Kari noted in our recorded duoethnography, "I think we have managed to uncover new information for ourselves through talking about old issues. But now that we have new layers of experiences to contribute to our understanding of those old issues, it creates new meaning." The creation of new meaning is crucial in duoethnography for social transformation, because new meanings affect our present understanding of past experiences and thus our thoughts, knowledge, and behaviors in the social world. This process was also demonstrated by Claudia's realization (during our recorded duoethnography) in response to her written reflections:

> Reading our written reflections I noticed how certain structures in society can affect the perceptions, assumptions, and understandings of people (including children) and can influence how social groups relate each other in terms of values, rights, and social justice. In my case my transition from a private school to a public one made me be aware of social differences that I had not noticed clearly before.

Through our conversation and her writing, Claudia realized that her childhood conceptions of difference between the public and private school students and families had more to do with classism than with actual tangible socio-economic differences such as the quality of housing or the provision of healthcare. Her views on socio-economic difference were tainted by the discriminatory values that were projected on her by society. Claudia said,

> Now that I am talking to you I realized that what I thought, as a child, were big differences between my middle class neighbours and my working class classmates were profoundly accentuated by a framework that classified people by practices of distinction. I felt that there was something different about the nature of people, and now I realized how the discourses about class tinted my ideas about class difference.

Thus, as a result of the ongoing duoethnography sessions and reflective writing, she now views these differences through a new lens. These examples show the interplay between past and present and demonstrate how duoethnography contributes to a reconceptualization of sorts.

The possibility of transformation is also what makes duoethnography not only a methodology but also a pedagogy: "In this way duoethnography is a form of research but for me it is a form of pedagogy—like teaching ourselves and each other through conversations and the development of new meaning." Here, Kari expressed how duoethnography seems to reacquaint the researcher and the learner with content that matters—content that is so frequently bracketed out of the realm of research and dismissed for its emotionality, its subjectivity, its fallibility. We suggest here not that duoethnography can or should replace the forms of research and pedagogy that currently occupy the sphere of influence in graduate programs, but that it can be used to contest aspects of systemic and structural restrictions that are excessively focused on functionality and productivity. This way of learning and challenging renders the learner a unique expression of historical, social–emotional, and political contexts, among others.

Analysis: Duoethnography as Curriculum and Pedagogy

In alignment with the method of currere, we develop the analysis of our written and polyvocal texts by applying four steps of currere, as described by William Pinar (2010): (1) regressive, (2) progressive, (3) analytical, and (4) synthetical. As applied to our duoethnography, we carried out the regressive step through our weekly sessions by focusing on our identities (i.e., as a child, as a volunteer in Ghana, as undergraduate students) in relation to our conceptions and experiences of privilege. In a continuous dialectical exercise, we then examined our future identities as scholars, freely unpacking our desires and expectations of the kind of scholars of social justice we aspire to. In the analytic step, we examined both past experiences of privilege and future expectations of becoming an integral scholar of social justice. Finally, we developed a transformed attitude toward self-mobilization in the public sphere that we discuss further in this section.

As may be understood, these four steps are not linear in nature, but rather they are recursive. They are developed as a continuous collaborative exercise that gradually helped to uncover the multiple layers of our inquiry. We understood duoethnography as a method of inquiry that by itself is a contestation of an excessive and sometimes exclusive attention to the present moment that has allowed the maximization of curriculum of functionality. As this process of four steps shows, what we examine in the present is rooted in a complex temporal structure in which the boundaries of past and future overlap with the present. We structure our analysis around three key concepts that illuminate duoethnography's potential as a pedagogy and curriculum: Duoethnography as a complicated conversation and duoethnography as a tool for problematizing binaries.

Duoethnography: A Complicated Conversation

In keeping with the concept of currere, we understood our duoethnography as a complicated conversation in which, as graduate students, we drew on our autobiographies to develop a situated curriculum in a particular time (graduate school) and place (a Western university). What makes this conversation complex is the contestation of what Pinar calls presentism, an over-emphasis on the present moment, and a concurrent under-acknowledgment of the history behind our curriculum, and the people and structures that influenced its development. Our conversation responds to our dissatisfaction with the curricular content's limited ability to help us connect to our identities as scholars of social justice within a community of practice. We acknowledged that we had a leading role in that dissatisfaction, and, as a result, we challenged ourselves to change our ideas. This duoethnographic conversation offered us two levels of complexity: the complexity of examining the self and the temporal complexity that decenters the focus from the present moment.

A conversation about our autobiographies may be critiqued as overly self-indulgent and a re-centering of the privileged researcher; however, in duoethnography, the self (and we would argue, the self's discomfort) is understood as the *site* of research as opposed to the *topic* of research (Sawyer & Norris, 2013). In a way that is consistent with curriculum theory, we challenge the curriculum of higher education by shifting the focus from a production of disciplinary content or knowledge to an exploration of our discomfort in building our identity as scholars. We drew on our autobiographies as valid and trustful means to examine our lived experience in curricular conversation. As sites rather than subjects of our research, we examined our assumptions and interrogated our identities, exploring the interplay between former and future selves. Kari pointed out: "I think we have managed to uncover new information for ourselves through talking about old issues—but now that we have new layers of experiences to contribute to our understanding of those old issues, it creates new meaning." In approaching our research this way, we challenged presentism by "self-consciously cultivating the temporal structures of subjectivity, a lived complexity in which difference does not dissolve onto a flatted presentistic social surface" (Pinar, 2010, p. 179).

Duoethnography provided us with the methodological tools to carry on the examination of ourselves. When we started our weekly sessions, we had a contradictory feeling in which, on the one hand, we knew this conversation was crucial for our identity development, but, on the other hand, we felt it was separate from academic knowledge. However, through this process we realized that contrary to our assumptions, the academic (theoretical, pragmatic) content and the personal (emotional, historical) content were intimately intertwined and not tidily polarized, as is often suggested in false binaries between the intellectual and the emotional. As Claudia recalled about the duoethnographic process: "Although we put ourselves in the middle of the conversations, what we did was decenter the subject because we did not talk about ourselves or our dispositions." We talked finally how discourses about class, gender, whiteness, and privilege played out through ourselves. We put ourselves as material or artefact of our analysis." Our histories and how we described them contained larger societal discourses which were related somehow to narratives of superiority and oppression (Said, 1993) embedded in historical and cultural contexts.

In the everyday of these particular contexts, individuals internalize practices of dominance. We realized through sharing our historical narratives the degree to which we had internalized notions of dominance and privilege. Although at the onset of our conversations we focused on our personal experiences, the process of critical collaboration seemed to invoke an attention to the institutional, national, and transnational structures undergirding our perspectives (Sawyer & Norris, 2013), and in some cases, we became aware of how those structures and our positionality within them threaten our aspiration for a continual pursuit of scholarly integrity. Working collaboratively allowed us to identify those narratives, question and challenge them as a way of resisting dominant discourses. We did not emerge from our exhaustive conversations as the same learners we had once been; instead, a counter-discourse emerged that provided us the grounds to bring forward in academic discussion academics' autobiographies as needed sources for making sense and contesting knowledge.

This complicated conversation was possible because of our commitment to each other in building a trustful space for our interactions as the distinctive duoethnography's principle of ethics. We knew that in order to face the discomfort, we had to delve into memories that could be painful, and that could render us vulnerable to one another. This commitment to a reflexivity that not only looks at the self but also examines the self's assumptions and complicity in a larger web of interconnection laid a vital foundation for our project because it required trust between us as colleagues. Thus, the complexity of our duoethnography project was premised on a healthy respect for one another's vulnerability, and it allowed us to illuminate a key source of our discomfort: the unnecessary construction of binaries.

Duoethnography: A Tool for Problematizing Binaries

Early in our duoethnography sessions, we encountered the problematic nature of our binary construction, and the way that these binaries impose a contradiction between becoming scholars of integrity in our privileged contexts. We illustrate this tension through Kari's metaphor of a push-and-pull struggle between the idealist and the critic. Over the course of our three-month project, our conception of this tension shifted: Where we once felt ashamed or paralyzed, our naming of the problem helped us to mobilize it. Referring to these encounters, Claudia stated,

> This is the connection that I see between your tension and mine, is that we both felt kind of ashamed of being in that privileged position when we want to research topics of disadvantage. So in that sense, the movement that you did between opposite binaries, like you said between the idealist and the critic, is very important to illustrate how these feelings of shame affect our understanding of researcher identity.

We sought to locate the in-between spaces of the two opposing voices (the idealist and the critic) and we stayed there as long as possible. Considering how duoethnography helped us as a methodology for self-examination, Kari reflected,

> and for me it was important to feel that connection, or at least try to understand how I can reconcile all the ideas of the idealist within me, with a lot

> of the literature and my cognitive and emotional alignment with the critic, especially around social justice or the work that we do in our department.

Examining the in-between spaces week after week allowed us the use of duoethnography to consistently build new and ongoing ways of examining ourselves:

> I feel that through our conversations, it is like we have become better equipped to frame our privilege differently and to talk through the points that were really holding us back. … But through talking about it I sort of started to understand how I can reconcile being a white privileged woman from the west with doing research about ethical international engagement, particularly around international service learning. But it has always been a struggle for me, and it should remain a struggle, because to be doing this work, we should always be critiquing our own positionality and the ways that we're complicit in inequality. It's important to note that understanding our own complicity doesn't necessarily lead to change, but it does comprise an essential element of political action. But this duoethnography series has been formative for me; I still remember what you said when we were talking about—that I don't have to choose between these two stands, that I do not have one or the other in this binary. And from that, we began talking about our physical reactions and physical feelings related to these tensions—like feeling the struggle in the pit of our stomach; it opened up a new line of inquiry I hadn't thought too deeply about before.

We intentionally discussed the problematization and observation of binaries rather than a balancing of binaries. As Claudia pointed out, "trying to stay in the middle of those two identities (the idealist and the critic) is not about balance; it is about understanding that there is an important thing that is happening between them that it has to do with, for example, interconnectedness." Kari added, "and that the tension and the conversation in between the two of them is ongoing and it is not meant to end." In the simplest of terms, we realized through this project that the very things we were fighting to "resolve" and "overcome"—the discomfort and the tension—were a great source of our learning and, especially in the work of social justice, were *supposed to be there*. Megan Boler's "pedagogy of discomfort" is helpful here for highlighting the essential role of binaries in opening up spaces for learning and creativity: "The recognition of our ethical dilemmas as 'intrinsically paradoxical,' the recognition that contradictory beliefs and desires may coexist, provides creative spaces to inhabit"

(p. 197). She contends that rather than trying to resolve these paradoxes, we "take discomfort as an approach: an approach to how we see"; extending this, Boler suggests that in doing so, we learn to "bear witness to ourselves" as a way of both teaching and learning (p. 197).

Problematizing these binaries helped us to observe, reframe and extend our inquiry around what it means to be a graduate student and researcher in relation to our lived histories and personal identities. Our duoethnographic conversations have aided in our unlearning of fixed ideas of privilege, so that where once our question was, "How can I be a researcher and educator in this field when I understand my privileged position as an embodiment or an expression of inequality?," now our questions might instead be, "What is my narrative and my identity, and how can my positionality serve my contribution? How might I ensure that my work is guided by an ongoing critique of my privilege and unequal power structures, without allowing the inner critic to halt my work altogether? How can I bear witness to the binaries I construct and how might this in-between space inform my work as a scholar?" We realized that on a daily basis we had been constructing these binaries, and, through our project, we also observed how we had done so as Claudia said: "I have seen myself reproducing the same fixed categories that we have examined through these conversations in day-to-day situations, and now because of our conversations my aspiration is to be aware of and change that. Now I think that I will be more aware of those binaries."

Concluding Remarks

Through our own experience with duoethnography as a learning tool, we hope to have illustrated its potential methodologically, pedagogically, and in terms of curriculum, specifically, in this case, graduate studies. In particular, we ourselves gained benefits in these arenas through the development of a sense of community and identity, which was brought about through duoethnographic conversations. While two people do not a community make, we used the methodology to build a sense of intimacy and vulnerability with one another, but we also continuously carry the learnings with us into many spaces in the university and beyond. This project therefore helped us bridge our personal narratives with academic knowledge. While this project has been helpful for its bridging qualities on a personal level and in building a sense of intimacy in our immediate scholarly community, we also acknowledge the limits of its effectiveness within a highly traditional and structured institution: vulnerability and emotion have long been marginalized within academia, and, in some senses, duoethnography risks endangering participants' perceived value in a system that rewards rationality, sureness, and infallibility. Duoethnography, of course, is antithetical to all three of these concepts: Its intimate nature often raises emotions, thoughts, and ineffable issues that fall outside the realm of rational understanding; its personal and reflective qualities can unearth critical self-examination that is too often seen as a problem of self-doubt or a lack of confidence in one's knowledge; and, finally, the vulnerable aspect of duoethnography insists upon an honest inquiry into our fallibility and the strategies and ideas that "fail" to serve our goals and the goals of communities we serve. So it is with caution that we uphold duoethnography as a strategy for building an intimate sense of community within an institutional landscape that appears to work toward dissonant goals from those we propose in this chapter. Nonetheless, we contend that, when used creatively, duoethnography may be integrated into a graduate program to assist students with conversations that examine assumptions, histories, and personal relationships to societal structures. However, we do not propose that duoethnography is a cure-all solution to a much larger, more complex problem within academia; instead, it can be thought of as one strategy or starting point in the quest for a graduate education program that is marked by vulnerability, intimate community relationships, and enlightening fallibility. By sharing narratives with one another in face-to-face dialogue, students may be further encouraged to reflect upon their own tensions in the graduate journey, and how these tensions relate to their absorption of the standardized curriculum. While serving to teach students about themselves and their relationship to curriculum, duoethnography can also develop a sense of community and alleviate some of the issues of isolation that are shown to so negatively affect graduate student achievement.

Inspired by the idea that conversations, duoethnographic or otherwise, are not merely rooted in the present but are rather continuous and ever-transforming, we conclude not with anything "tidy" or definitive. Instead, we hope our narrative serves as a jumping-off point for extended discussions around the use of duoethnography as a methodology and simultaneously as a helpful tool in using curriculum and pedagogy to contest aspects of an education system that does not serve the broader goals of social justice. What began as a spark of discomfort in our graduate program fueled a curiosity around our identities, our lived histories, and their role in our capacity to learn a standardized curriculum while also finding our scholarly voices. We used duoethnography as a learning tool on a weekly basis, and discovered that our discomfort, which resulted from paradoxical, binary identities, ought not be banished but, rather, ought to be observed and celebrated as a space of learning—a space that is meant to be contested, emotional, and ambiguous in any field, but especially in the realm of social justice. It is quite likely that as long as social structures continue to value profit and functionality over justice, we will continue to feel the tensions raised here; however, duoethnography provides a tool within the current system for critical conversation and political contestation.

References

Aujla-Bhullar, S., & Grain, K. (2010). Mirror imagining diversity experiences: A juxtaposition of identities in cross-cultural initiatives. In L. Darren, R. Sawyer, & J. Norris (Eds.), *Duoethnography: Dialoguic methods for social, health, and educational research* (pp. 199–222). Walnut Creek, CA: Left Coast Press.

Chang, H. (2008). *Autoethnography as method*. Walnut Creek, CA: Left Coast Press.

Cotterall, S. (2013). More than just a brain: Emotions and the doctoral experience. *Higher Education Research & Development, 32*(2), 174–187.

Devenish, R., Dyer, S., Jefferson, T., Lord, L., Leeuwen, S., & Fazakerley, V. (2009). Peer to peer support: The disappearing work in the doctoral student experience. *Higher Education Research & Development, 28*(1), 59–70.

Gearing, R. E. (2008). Bracketing. In Given, L.M. (Ed.), *Sage encyclopedia of qualitative research methods* (pp. 233–236). Sage Publications.

McAlpine, L., & Norton, J. (2006). Reframing our approach to doctoral programs: An integrative framework for research and action. *Higher Education Research & Development, 25*(1), 3–17.

Ng-A-Fook, N., & Milne, R. (2014). Unsettling our narrative encounters within and outside of Canada Social Studies. *Canadian Social Studies, 47*(2), 88–109.

Norris, J. (2008). Duoethnography. In Given, L.M. (Ed.), *Sage encyclopedia of qualitative research methods* (pp. 233–236). Sage Publications. doi:10.4135/9781412963909

Norris, J., Sawyer, R., & Lund, D. E. (2012). *Duoethnography: Dialogic methods for social, health, and educational research*. Walnut Creek, CA: Left Coast Press.

Pinar, W. (1975). Currere: Toward reconceptualization. In W. F. Pinar (Ed.), *Curriculum theorizing: The reconceptualists* (pp. 396–414). Berkeley, CA: McCutchan.

Pinar, W. (1978). Notes on the curriculum field 1978. *Educational Researcher, 7*(8), 5–12.

Pinar, W. (2010). Currere. In Kridel, C. (Ed.), *Encyclopedia of curriculum studies.* Sage Publications. doi:10.4135/9781412958806.n102

Pinar, W. (2011, October). Allegories of the present: Curriculum development in a culture of narcissism and presentism (Keynote address to the Opening Plenary). In *First International Congress on Curriculum and Instruction*, Eskisehir.

Potts, K., & Brown, L. (2005). Becoming an anti-oppressive researcher. In L. Brown & S. Strega (Eds.), *Research as resistance: Critical, indigenous, and anti-oppressive approaches* (pp. 255–283). Toronto, ON: Canadian Scholars' Press/Women's Press.

Said, E. (1993). *Culture and imperialism.* New York: Alfred A. Knoff.

Sawyer, R., & Norris, J. (2013). *Duoethnography: Understanding qualitative research.* New York, NY: Oxford University Press.

Thomson, P., & Walker, M. (Eds.). (2010). *Routledge doctoral student's companion: Getting to grips with research in education and the social sciences.* New York, NY: Routledge.

Index[1]

[1] Note: Page numbers with "n" denote endnotes.

J. Norris, *Theorizing Curriculum Studies, Teacher Education, and Research through Duoethnographic Pedagogy*,
DOI 10.1057/978-1-137-51745-6